Quiet Shouts

Louise Stoltzfus

Quiet Shouts

Stories of
Lancaster
Mennonite
Women
Leaders

Louise
Stoltzfus

Foreword by
Paul M. Zehr

A Pandora Press U.S. Book

**Herald
Press**

Scottdale, Pennsylvania
Waterloo, Ontario

Library of Congress Cataloging-in-Publication Data
Stoltzfus, Louise, 1952-
Quiet Shouts : stories of Lancaster Mennonite women leaders / Louise
Stoltzfus ; foreword by Paul M. Zehr.
    p.   cm.
    "A Pandora Press U.S. book"
    Includes bibliographical references.
    ISBN 0-8361-9116-1 (alk. paper)
    1. Women missionaries Biography. 2. Mennonite women Biogra-
phy. 3. Mennonite Church. Lancaster Conference Biography. 4. Mis-
sionaries Biography. 5. Mennonites Biography. I. Title
BV2545.S76 1999
289.7'092'274815—dc21
[B]   99-22054
                                                                  CIP

The paper used in this publication is recycled and meets the minimum
requirements of American National Standard for Information
Sciences—Permanence of Paper for Printed Library Materials, ANSI
Z39.48-1984.

Except when otherwise marked, all Bible quotations are from the King
James Version of the BIble. Passages marked NIV are from the Holy
Bible: New International Version. Copyright © 1973, 1978, 1984
International Bible Society. Used by permission of Zondervan Bible
Publishers. All rights reserved.

QUIET SHOUTS
Copyright © 1999 by Herald Press, Scottdale, Pa. 15683
        Published simultaneously in Canada by Herald Press,
        Waterloo, Ont. N2L 6H7. All rights reserved
Website: www.mph.org
Library of Congress Catalog Number: 99-22054
International Standard Book Number: 0-8361-9116-1
Printed in the United States of America
Book design by Gwen M. Stamm, Herald Press, in collaboration with
Michael A. King, Pandora Press U.S.
Cover design by Gwen M. Stamm, Herald Press

08 07 06 05 04 03 02 01 00 99 10 9 8 7 6 5 4 3 2 1

To Marilyn Kennel,
Who believed in me and this project
from the beginning

Contents

Foreword

QUIET SHOUTS IS MUST READING for North American Mennonites. Embedded in these true stories of Mennonite women is an overview of the twentieth-century experience of Lancaster Mennonite Conference congregations and members. What began as a turn-of-the-century revival among these eastern Pennsylvania Mennonites moved by midcentury toward a legalistic stranglehold. Then in the last third of the century, the winds of the Holy Spirit caused new life to break out. Women lived these themes more than men, and the stories in this book take one into the reality of these experiences.

This book gives insight into the missionary movement among Lancaster Conference Mennonites by looking through the eyes of women deeply involved in overseas and home missions. One senses the excitement experienced as women prayed, then found God leading them to the mission field. One also feels the strain of restraint placed on many of these women by godly men trying to work within the culture and ecclesiology of that day. Reading this book will open eyes to the great hand of God breaking through in the lives of ordinary people who, through their parents' influence, and sometimes their congregations' encouragement, experienced God's call into kingdom work.

As we enter the twenty-first century another revival is taking place. This revival is gradually opening insights into the New Testament regarding women in ministry which will, no doubt, bring change to the church for the next century. New Testament evangelical scholars such as F. F. Bruce, Gordon Fee, James D. G. Dunn, Mary J. Evans, Craig S. Keener, Mary Stewart Van Leeuwen, Stanley Grenz, and E. Earl Ellis all have shown the New Testament church not only taught women can be involved in ministry, but also showed by practice in the New Testament this was the case. Evangelical scholars like Ben Witherington have shown that Galatians 3:27-28 was a baptismal formula used by the early church. The New Testament church felt so deeply about the gospel changing people's lives by the power of the crucified and resurrected Lord that the barriers of race, economics, and gender dare not stand in the way of God's work of reconciliation in the world.

It is fitting, therefore, that the stories in this book come to light, for in them we discover the hand of God both in thrusting women into mission and in calling them to leadership roles. These accounts are not unlike the experience of the New Testament church.

Louise Stoltzfus, who gathered these chapters and wrote them in their final form, is to be congratulated for the quality of her work. With the encouragement of the Women in Leadership Subcommittee of the Leadership Council of the Lancaster Mennonite Conference, Louise has given us a fine book.

I commend *Quiet Shouts* to you as a source of insight into what God has done and is now doing among us. As readers we are invited to join God's great work and reverently thank God for leading these women, as well as many others whose stories have not yet been told, in God's great reconciling mission in the world.

—*Paul M. Zehr*
October 1998

Acknowledgments

ON BEHALF OF THE Women in Leadership Subcommittee (WILS), who envisioned and directed this project, I thank those members of the Lancaster Mennonite Conference who have long advocated for women with leadership gifts.

More active and concentrated efforts to bring these women and their stories to the attention of conference leaders began in the 1980s with a group called Friends of Mutuality. By May 1982 this group had become the Task Force on Women in Church and Family, a committee officially formed by the conference to study women's issues. Inspired by the tireless efforts of Friends of Mutuality, the task force completed an extensive survey on beliefs and practices of Lancaster Conference women in August 1983. When the task force ended its work in October 1991, they passed the baton to WILS, a group organized to offer support on women's issues to the Leadership Council of the Lancaster Mennonite Conference.

Out of WILS came the vision for this book. Special thanks thus are owed to the six original WILS members—Marilyn Kennel, Clyde Kratz, Lois Nafziger, Donna Mack Shenk, A. Grace Shenk, and Paul Zehr. In particular, Paul Zehr's undying enthusiasm for the project and Marilyn Kennel's second-mile work on the early research made my task much easier.

I would also like to thank those additional WILS members who served after I signed on to do the writing in March 1997—Priscilla Garrett, Jason Kuniholm, Carol Oberholtzer,

Mary Yunginger Rittenhouse, and Ruth Weaver. In particular, Ruth Weaver's direction as chair of WILS and her faithful emotional support for me proved invaluable as I struggled through the hard stages of writing about other women's lives. Special thanks to Carol Oberholtzer for guiding the work of the editorial committee who read the manuscript and offered much helpful advice. Thanks to Sue Aeschliman Groff, Nathan Hege, Janet Kreider, and Glen Roth who joined Carol for this important part of the process.

Other people to whom I turned for advice and support include Doug Burkholder, Doris Kolb, Maribel Kraybill, Jerry Peters, Joanne Hess Siegrist, Mildred Steffy, Michael and Alonna Sprunger, A. Grace Wenger, and Chester and Sara Jane Wenger. I also thank Lancaster Mennonite Historical Society for making its archives so accessible to me. Special thanks to Steve Ness, who helped me search for many boxes of archival material, and Carolyn Charles Wenger for making the library a truly great center for research about the Lancaster Mennonite Conference. A collection of materials gathered during the research of this book will be donated to the Historical Society. It includes the written stories of many women who were not included in *Quiet Shouts*.

My highest gratitude goes to the fourteen women whose stories are told in this book. I especially thank those living at the time of this writing. Their open and willing sharing transformed how I thought about Mennonite women in leadership. I thank them for allowing me to tell in-progress stories, knowing that by the time of publication details of their personal narrative would have changed. May God bless each one.

WILS also wishes to thank the thirty-nine individuals and several churches whose generous financial contributions made this book possible.

—*Louise Stoltzfus*

Author's Preface

AS I WAS WRITING THIS BOOK, an unexpected phenomenon occurred. The list of women whose stories needed to be told grew by leaps and bounds. Whenever I described the project, people invariably began asking or telling me about specific women. Was she in the book? Would her story be told? Did I know about their mother? Their Sunday school teacher? The church planter? The evangelist? It soon became apparent that there were dozens of Lancaster Mennonite women whose stories belonged in this twentieth-century review of women in leadership.

Some of the women described to me labored patiently behind the scenes for many years, giving Lancaster Conference-related congregations the best part of their many-layered lives. Some were overshadowed by better-known husbands. Some sought fulfillment in other careers, working as nurses, teachers, and small business owners. Some left the conference, finding open doors in other denominations and other Mennonite Church conferences. All lived with a tradition that asked them to be quiet. Nevertheless, they also found ways to shout.

Many additional women leaders continue to fill pastoral roles in Lancaster Conference churches. Some are recognized, some not. A few have deaconess credentials; many others are content as lay leaders. Women with and without credentials bring blessing and hope to the countless people who enter the doors of mainstream and far-afield Lancaster Conference congregations. Along with male counterparts, these women extend God's grace and love to their own people and the world, con-

veying the church's promised ministry of healing and reconciliation in Jesus Christ.

Among contemporary Lancaster Conference leaders are
four women in addition to Lena Horning Brown (see chapter 9)
whose names were submitted to the Bishop Board for ordination during 1998—Nadine Smith-Bulford, Mercedes Gonzalez,
Theda Good, and Ruth Wenger. At the 1998 Fall Conference
Meeting held at Weaverland Mennonite Church, the three bishops who represented these women stood and gave impassioned
pleas for the conference to resolve its position regarding the ordination of women. The bishops requested permission to grant
ministerial credentials to the women, each of whom actively
serves in a pastorate directed by the Lancaster Conference.

Monroe Yoder, the bishop of the New York City district,
spoke for both Mercedes Gonzalez and Ruth Wenger, pastor of
North Bronx Mennonite Church. He named Mercedes and told
her story. In 1979 two of her sons-in-law were serving as pastors
of Iglesia Unida de Avivamiento in Brooklyn, one of nineteen
Mennonite churches in New York City. Mercedes agreed to become a church-appointed missionary, assigned to make regular
home and hospital visits.

A gray-haired grandmother with a fire for evangelism and
the work of the church, Mercedes said yes when several people
she was discipling asked her to pastor a small, independent Pentecostal congregation in the neighborhood. The pastor had
gone to Puerto Rico for several months. When the pastor returned, the congregation pled for Mercedes to remain in leadership because she had "mothered them into the church."

Due to her connections to Avivamiento, Mercedes approached the Lancaster Conference Mennonites for help in
making the decision. Monroe negotiated a settlement with the
Pentecostal leaders, and a Mennonite church planting was born.
Located in the Bushwick section of Brooklyn, Iglesia Cristiana

Valle de Jesus ministers to about 100 people, many of them neighborhood children and young people. The New York Council of Mennonite Churches recognizes Mercedes as pastor of the congregation, and the Lancaster Conference calls her a church planter. Her congregation has requested that she be given pastoral credentials.

Freeman Miller, bishop of the Philadelphia district, spoke for Nadine Smith-Bulford. With her husband, Charles, Nadine pastors New Mercies Mennonite Church in the East Falls section of Philadelphia. A fifth-generation woman pastor, Nadine holds ministerial credentials in the Church of God in Christ, the United Holy Church, and the United Pentecostal Council of the Assemblies of God. Sent to the Mennonites by the Church of God in Christ, Nadine and Charles are passionate about the mission at New Mercies "to become a refuge of mercy that will care for sinners and those sinned against, to proclaim salvation through Jesus Christ, and provide a wholistic ministry that will disciple and empower individuals, families, and communities."

Harold Reed, bishop of the Lancaster City district, spoke for Theda Good, a member of the pastoral team at ACTS Covenant Fellowship. The congregations requesting ordination for these four women, however, are far from traditional Mennonite churches. Each has a passion for the poor and for bringing people into the presence of God who might not feel at home in old-style Mennonite country churches.

The tension between the city churches each of the four women represent and the rural Mennonite leaders to whom they look for credentials echo stresses evident earlier in the twentieth century. Some of the struggles these women face are a mirror image of the search for understanding that emanated from the Philadelphia Home Mission in the 1910s and 1920s, the Tanganyika Mennonite Church in the 1930s and 1940s, and the Diamond Street Mennonite Church in the 1950s and 1960s.

Just as their forebears prayed for the women of the Philadelphia Home Mission, the church in Tanganyika, and the people at Diamond Street, women and men in today's Lancaster Conference also pray for God's direction and wisdom to touch both the women leaders and those who must make the difficult decisions about ordination and the church of tomorrow.

By design, this book has no concluding chapter. That chapter will be written by others as God continues the all-consuming work of regeneration and renewal around the question of women in leadership. Perhaps the few stories told here will become a jumping-off point for scholars and researchers to discover women leaders—both young and old—in Lancaster Mennonite Conference and beyond.

—*Louise Stoltzfus*
Lancaster, Pennsylvania

Quiet Shouts

Amanda Musselman

1

Highly Favored among Women

Amanda Musselman
Philadelphia, Pennsylvania

NORTH AMERICAN MENNONITES at the close of the nineteenth century stood on the brink of a new era. Having lived as unassuming, quiet-in-the-land farmers and homemakers for nearly two centuries, they encountered a great spiritual awakening in the late 1800s. Revival swept across the wheat fields and tobacco patches, swirled through the kitchens and parlors, and swayed from the pulpits, down the aisles, and around the edges of nearly every new-world Mennonite community.

Preachers stopped using the traditional, sing-song German. They began speaking English, evoking the bliss of heaven and the horror of hell in language that made both old and young reach for the right and quake before the wrong. Sunday schools spawned controversies between conservative and progressive church elements but also introduced Bible-centered discussion and extemporaneous prayer. Evening revival meetings, called "protracted meetings" because they lasted as long as the evangelist and local leaders felt led, brought long lines of buggies and thousands of people to the small-town and country churches.

Many dramatic changes occurred, some instantly. That was how it was for Amanda Musselman in the summer of 1896.

Lancaster County Mennonites, known for their cautious conservatism, were slow to embrace the movement which had significantly altered several other Mennonite communities by the 1880s. People in Amanda's home congregation, the affluent Groffdale Mennonites of rural New Holland, expressed both openness and suspicion toward the evangelists and their call for regeneration and new life in Christ. Her own family was divided. Jacob Musselman, her father, sympathized with the progressive revival preachers. Her mother, Mary Stoner Musselman, did not appreciate or understand the groundswell of emotion and innovation that inspired this changing time.[1]

In the first years of the revival, Amanda remained aloof and largely unaffected. Tall and slender with just a tint of red in her upswept hair, she was a lovely young woman gliding through her mid-twenties. Known for her high spirits and penchant for stepping out with the sons of New Holland-area businessmen, many of them Mennonite, she continued to dress in the high Victorian fashions of the time while occasionally attending Sunday morning services at Groffdale.[2]

Then one Saturday evening in July 1896, twenty-six-year-old Amanda headed to a party with a group of friends.[3] Late that night, two of the young people present at the gathering—Enos Barge of Strasburg and Barbara Hershey of Paradise—were killed in a shattering train-buggy wreck at the railroad crossing in Bird-in-Hand. The accident became a lightning rod for the 1890s Lancaster County revival. Evangelists singled out the young, imploring them to change their ways before they too lost their lives and souls. In a move that exacerbated the pain for their families and friends, some preachers held up Enos and Barbie as examples of unrepentant sinners because, like many young people of the time, they had not yet joined the church.

Soon after the death of her friends, Amanda's father invited one of the traveling evangelists to his home, asking that he speak to the young-adult Musselman children about receiving Jesus. That night in her family home, the pleasures of the world lost their allure for Amanda Musselman. She applied for church membership. Three months after the accident—on October 31, 1896—Amanda and forty-two others were baptized at the Groffdale Mennonite meetinghouse. From that time forward, she was a changed person—changed in action, voice, and even appearance.

Shedding elegant dresses for plain clothing, as Amanda did, was championed by the leaders of this particular revival movement. Like many Mennonite young people in the waning years of the nineteenth century, Amanda had kept abreast of popular styles, often wearing lovely ensembles complete with fancy trimmings and hats.[4] She grew up during a time when the mainstream Lancaster Mennonite community had no uniform plain dress requirements. Children and youth could and did dress quite fashionably. After they were baptized into church membership, young men changed little. Women, on the other hand, commonly adjusted to wearing toned-down versions of current styles along with some type of plain head covering.

To avoid this rather cumbersome change as long as possible, many young women and men waited to be baptized until they were married. Some even waited for many years after marriage. Often carefree and experimental in their youth, many young Mennonites mingled easily with members of the larger society.

Into this culture rode the 1890s preachers of the Great Awakening. Although their primary interest was saving souls, they made the message of radical salvation more palatable for the older folks by clearly embracing Mennonite distinctives.[5] What this meant for women like Amanda Musselman must never be underestimated. Because she discarded her fashionable clothing on the day she received salvation and joined the church, she connected faithful living to plain dress for the rest of her life. So did many other Mennonites who came to personal faith in the years following the 1890s revival. Head coverings, cape dresses, and black stockings for women and plain-cut suits for men became interlocked with spirituality.

Plain dress was only one of several themes to grow out of the accents and inflections of revival preachers and, eventually, to distinguish the century for Lancaster Mennonites. The first and most recognizable of these recurring themes became known as the mission movement. Two years after her conversion, Amanda Musselman answered the call to Christ's vineyard when one of the Great Awakening's most influential personalities, Noah H. Mack, recommended her to the leaders of the 1896 Lancaster Mennonite Sunday School Mission (hereinafter referred to as the Sunday School Mission)—a lay-driven mission endeavor dedicated to planting Sunday schools throughout the region.

As the first Sunday school superintendent at Groffdale, Noah found Amanda's dedication inspiring. After her conversion, she took church life seriously, attending services regularly and supporting the congregation's growing emphasis on Christian witness. One Sunday morning a snowstorm kept many Groffdale folks home in their warm houses. Not Amanda: she walked several miles across the fields from the Musselman farm to the meetinghouse. As Noah Mack watched her approach, he told himself Amanda Musselman would be a good candidate for the mission field.[6]

The Sunday School Mission soon invited her to help pioneer a mission project in the Kensington Mills section of northeast Philadelphia. To prepare for the ambiance and reality of urban living, Amanda traveled to the Chicago Home Mission, a similar outreach directed by midwestern Mennonites, where she spent the winter of 1898-1899. There she joined Mary Denlinger, a native of Paradise, Pennsylvania. Mary came to personal faith some years before the religious fervor that engaged Lancastrians after the death of Enos Barge and Barbara Hershey. She went to Chicago when that mission opened in October 1894. By the time Amanda arrived on Christmas Day in 1898, Mary was already an old hand at city mission work. They became inseparable.[7]

As planned, the Lancaster Sunday School Mission sent the two women to the City of Brotherly Love on June 6, 1899. Amanda was twenty-nine; Mary was thirty-one. Their mandate was "visiting and comforting the sick, and relieving the wants of the deserving poor, and to let [your] lights shine in every possible way."[8] They moved into an unkempt house in a middle-class industrial neighborhood.

From the beginning, Amanda took charge. She scrubbed the house from attic to cellar, waging an aggressive war against the bugs, dirt, and grease. With Mary she planned the first Sunday school. On Sunday morning, June 11, they held classes in their home with one neighborhood child and about twenty interested Mennonite friends from the outlying rural communities. Though hoping for more local children by the next Sunday, Amanda and Mary rejoiced.[9] They believed that God had called them to this city community, and they determined to follow God no matter what challenges or frustrations the years might bring.

Indeed, one disappointment shadowed many of Amanda's days. Her mother objected to city mission work and was especially aggrieved that two young women would go off to the unknown dangers of urban life alone. Mary Stoner Musselman refused to add an amen to the blessing Amanda's father gave his daughter.[10]

In a letter to her sister Katie several days after she and Mary arrived at 1930 East York Street, Amanda reflected with considerable pain, "The morning I left home mother's nose was bleeding, and both pap and I were somewhat uneasy. I felt uneasy some days, thought if something would happen pap would not know where I was."[11] Later letters exposed a rift that would take years to heal. In September 1899 Amanda admonished Katie to "pray earnestly to the Father for mother" because of her "bitter opposition" to mission work.

Amanda longed for her mother's approval. She invited her parents to visit the mission, which they evidently never did. She penned several heavy-handed invitational letters filled with Scripture texts.[12] She described visits to the New Holland area that did not include time with her parents. "The people though almost strangers to us all treated us with great kindness and we realize that to leave anything for Christ's sake we reap a hundred fold," she wrote to her parents after one trip to the country.[13] On this journey home, Amanda and Mary rode the trolley directly past the Musselman homestead. "In passing your place I thought I saw Mother and a strange lady sitting in the kitchen and waved to father," she wrote in the same letter. "I didn't know if father knew me, or only waved because I waved."

Amanda's letters home suggest a reconciliation with her mother sometime shortly before or soon after her father's death in 1911. During the summer of 1916, Amanda made several visits to New Holland because her mother was not feeling well. After one train ride back to the city, she wrote, "I had a card from Mattie [her older sister] written on Monday telling me how you were but wonder so often, hope there will be someone with you all the time, and that you will get better."[14] Amanda and her mother appeared to be at peace.

A growing solemnity shaped Amanda's psyche as she matured. She abandoned the frivolity and fun of her twenties, becoming a sedate and sober mission worker by her fortieth birthday in October 1909. To her the work of God was paramount, and she exhibited intense personal piety. She was convinced that nothing—not her mother's questions, not the quickening pulse of city life—must come between her and God. She lived in Philadelphia because God called her to witness to the lost, to minister to those in sin, and to work at meeting needs of the poor.

In all aspects of Amanda's life, the spiritual superseded the natural. She quoted Scripture verses for nearly every situation, reading the Bible during a daily morning regimen of meditation and prayer. She lived Mennonite doctrine, encouraging the youngsters who came to the mission to adopt the plain way. Very few did. This too fit Amanda's philosophy that true Christianity required sacrifice and submission. Once, in a letter that also reveals she had not entirely lost her bright sense of humor, she wrote, "The Lord is permitting it to rain Sundays of late to prove how many of the Christians are weather proof."[15]

As the rural directors of the Sunday School Mission recommended, she traveled home to Groffdale to keep communion twice a year, staying in her sister Katie's home. There her niece, Ruth Myers Wyble, observed Amanda's piety. "She always came home on Friday evening. Then she would spend all day Saturday upstairs in her room fasting, praying, and reading. She didn't even come down for meals. On Sunday she went with us to communion at Groffdale. In those years when I was a child, I thought she was a very serious soul."

Ruth also remembers Amanda's gift for organization and her ability to get the job done. "I remember visiting the mission with my parents and thinking it was Aunt 'Manda who organized the work and Mary Denlinger who loved those children into the mission. They were a perfect pair. 'Manda was a little quicker, but they both were interested in saving the lost."[16]

Although the Sunday School Mission appointed Joseph Bechtel superintendent of the Philadelphia work, Amanda and

Mary ran the Philadelphia Home Mission. They lived on site; Joseph and his family did not. A contractor who had moved into the city from the rural Oley Valley, Joseph was a mild-mannered man whose primary energies went into his business and family. The Bechtels lived southwest of Kensington and much closer to the old city on Mt. Vernon Street. They enjoyed the "sister workers," as Amanda and Mary were called, and regularly attended Sunday school and other services at the mission. Joseph Bechtel carried the titles of superintendent and treasurer, but he clearly entrusted management of the city mission to Amanda and Mary.

For fourteen years, the sister workers enjoyed the largesse and support of surrounding rural communities with few eyebrows raised about how they did their work. The Philadelphia Home Mission flourished. Amanda and Mary conducted sewing classes on Saturdays, Sunday school on Sunday mornings, children's meeting and Bible study on Sunday evenings, Bible study on Tuesday evenings, and memory work on Thursday evenings.[17] They visited those suffering from illness and gave food and clothing to the poor. They made a concentrated effort to connect with Mennonites who had moved to the city, once reporting they had reached out to about fifty Mennonites, "including an invalid widow living in a two-room, third-floor apartment."[18] They hosted regular delegations from both the Franconia and Lancaster Mennonite communities.

Rural preachers took turns riding the rails to Philadelphia to conduct Sunday services, notes A. Grace Wenger, Amanda Musselman's biographer and an authority on her life and work. "Amanda always made a great show of deference to the ordained men appointed to travel to the city and 'help' with the Sunday morning services," says Wenger. "But she and Mary did the work. They did all the work. And of that pair, Amanda was definitely the dominant one."[19] Mary's affectionate, generous heart and Amanda's assertive, fix-it personality drew people to the work. They provided care and love for a struggling city neighborhood, consistently recording Sunday school attendance of more than one hundred children and letting their lights shine as they had been instructed.

Because the sister workers were volunteers, they did not enjoy a prescribed salary or operate under a board-planned budget. When the Sunday School Mission sent Amanda and Mary to the city, they planned for the work to receive direct contributions. In a descriptive *Herald of Truth* report on the opening of the city work, John H. Mellinger, president of the Sunday School Mission, explained, "The mission is under the general charge of the Mennonite Sunday School Mission of Lancaster county, and will be supported by it so far as it is not supported by private contributions. While any funds sent to the officers of the Sunday School Mission for its support will be applied to this purpose, we would advise that they be sent direct to the treasurer of the Mission, Joseph Bechtel, 1820 Mt. Vernon street, *or to the workers, 1930 East York street*" [italics added].[20]

Amanda and Mary accepted invitations to visit Lancaster and Franconia Conference Mennonites, soliciting gifts for the mission.[21] On at least one occasion, Amanda spoke publicly about the mission work. The Weaverland congregation described Amanda and Mary's visit to their Sunday school in the summer of 1899 by writing to the *Herald of Truth*, "Sister Amanda Musselman, who was laboring in the Chicago Mission last winter, was with us and delivered an impressive address to the school on mission work; it was listened to attentively."[22] Many of these folks, as well as friends and relatives of the two women, donated food, money, and supplies directly to the Philadelphia mission.[23]

Amanda's letters to her family indicate that she took charge of the donations that came to the mission. Although

John H. Mellinger and the rural Sunday School Mission officers considered Joseph Bechtel the treasurer, the sisters directed, if not managed, the Philadelphia mission treasury. Careful stewardship of the hundreds of freewill offerings delivered to the mission became a matter of integrity and pride.

Neither Amanda nor Mary ever would have spoken in such terms, but many of their regular *Herald of Truth* reports show that they were both accomplished financial managers. February 1, 1900: "We too have found Philemon 4:19 to be true as several times when we thought we would have to draw from the Board, donations came from unknown sources." July 1, 1900: "Only a few times has the Lancaster county S. S. Mission (under whose direction we work) had the privilege of helping pay expenses." A year later, A. C. Kolb of Elkhart, Indiana, visited the mission. He reported, "The workers told me that thus far they have never yet been in want. In every case the Lord provided in time to make their payments promptly."

As volunteer workers, the sisters occasionally turned to an independent source of wealth. The Musselman family had invested in New Holland Machine stock, and they were not wanting for money.[24] Several times, Amanda asked her sister Katie to send "my interest money." She explained that having her own money to fall back on made her feel more secure.[25] Lina Zook Ressler, a friend of Amanda and Mary from their Chicago days, described the volunteer missionary's dilemma: "It was not unusual in those days for the missionary to take the last penny from her own personal pocketbook to buy bread for some poor family, because she knew that the reason the children had no bread was because the father drank up all his wages. Sister Amanda's tender heart found many needy, sorrowing hearts to help."[26]

Early in the summer of 1901, the Philadelphia Home Mission moved out of the East York site to a rental property at the corner of Amber and Dauphin, two and a half squares east. Six years later when this location also became overcrowded, the Sunday School Mission purchased one of the mansions near Norris Square, just north of the Kensington Mills industrial district.[27] The city mission's palatial new property at 2151 North Howard Street sat squarely in the demarcation zone between the rich factory owners and their struggling laborers. "Our next neighbors in the mansion, two widows, sisters, are going away to the seashore today for the summer, leaving their beautiful home to a servant and their brother, while back of them our next neighbors in the rear are the poor, who through poverty are compelled to stay in the heat of the city for the summer," Amanda wrote to her parents in 1910.[28]

Amanda and Mary turned each of their successive mission residences into an island of grace. The sister workers were accomplished cooks and housekeepers, and their home was, first of all, an oasis for them.[29] It was also a source of love to the neighborhood and the thousands of rural Mennonites who visited Philadelphia during Amanda and Mary's twenty-five-year sojourn in this eastern seaboard city.

On January 26, 1905, Amanda wrote to her parents, "Surely we are highly favored among women, kept by the power of God as the apple of his eye." On February 9, 1905, the workers thanked the mission's benefactors in their *Herald of Truth* report by proclaiming, "Could the donors have seen the happy families, supplied with a chicken, potatoes, apples and many other good things for a Christmas dinner, they would better understand the meaning of Jesus' words, 'It is more blessed to give than to receive.'"

On July 10, 1919, one rural Mennonite visitor expressed his own thanks in the church paper, now called *Gospel Herald*, "[We thank] the sisters at the Philadelphia Mission for giving us such a home-like atmosphere in which to live during those few days in which we made much more trouble than is paid for by any board bill that may be paid."[30]

These two highly favored women turned the edge of a decaying city neighborhood into a gracious and hospitable place. Filled with Swiss-South German Mennonite food, quilts, sewing projects, solid furniture, and simple decorations, their home was an inviting and pleasant space. The donations of committed patrons, the kind and wise counsel of Joseph Bechtel, the spiritual input from visiting preachers, and the occasional physical help from young Mennonite men who boarded with them combined to give the women a sense of wholeness and peace.

As early as 1914, however, the ground began to shift. John H. Mellinger transferred his considerable mission energies to a new governing board, Eastern Mennonite Board of Missions and Charities (hereinafter referred to as Eastern Board, though today called Eastern Mennonite Missions). From that time, the Sunday School Mission, which continued under new leadership until 1917, gradually lost its sense of purpose and vision.[31]

The Sunday School Mission's lay-driven quarterly meetings appealed to both women and men. Especially in the early days, women came forward at the meetings, responding to the call for workers as regularly as men. In those days, the Lancaster Conference Bishop Board was little more than an informal support group for the five to seven men who served this relatively small Mennonite community. Reflecting the concerns of various members of their community, some of the bishops were suspicious of the revival movement and mission activity. They stayed aloof, even wondering at first whether they could allow the 1896 lay mission movement.[32]

By 1914 loyalties among Lancaster Mennonites had changed dramatically. The ten-member Bishop Board, now organized as a decision-making body, had itself become mission-minded. They founded the new Eastern Board, offering their full blessing to John H. Mellinger. In a radical departure from the Sunday School Mission's lay-driven processes, John and his fellow visionaries responded by agreeing to check all future decisions with the bishops.

The Eastern Board's first order of business was to gather the diverse Lancaster projects—a number of outreach Sunday schools, a children's home, an industrial mission, an old people's home, and the Philadelphia Home Mission—into a stable structure and under one treasury and umbrella.[33] It worked; most of the mission outreach centers quickly agreed, looking forward to regular disbursement of funds from a central office. The Home Mission in Philadelphia, however, was not so eager.

Given their passion for volunteer city mission work, Amanda Musselman and Mary Denlinger may have found accounts of early Eastern Board meetings disturbing and strange. At the original August 11, 1914 meeting, two resolutions shed light on what would become the prevailing concerns of this board. First, the small group of men determined to build up the "weak and needy in the rural districts." Second, they discouraged direct gifts to mission locations by clearly stating that "money intended for mission and charitable purposes [should be] sent to and forwarded through this board."

At a later meeting, John W. Weaver spoke on "The Volunteer Missionary Problem." He declared, "The problem is solved in the word of God" and urged the church to ordain and send *men* to the field. A year and a half later, the same question still worried the group, and Amos Horst asked, "Has the Lancaster Co. Conference sent out a man on mission work?"[34] The sisters and Joseph Bechtel stayed loyal to their founding body—the Sunday School Mission, attending its continuing quarterly meetings. They also kept their treasury under on-site control.[35]

The fault line extending between Lancaster and the Philadelphia mission slowly became more and more unstable. Now in their early fifties, the plain and simple sister workers had not experienced city life without scars. The 1910 Philadelphia streetcar riots invaded their neighborhood. When Amanda stepped outside to investigate, she watched in consternation and shock as a crowd attacked the trolley, throwing stones and other objects through its windows. "There were women and children on the car," she wrote home, adding that people had been injured and killed in the transit company dispute.[36]

Violence returned to Kensington during the early 1920s union uprisings, and Mary saw a man kicked to death as he got off the streetcar near the mission. The mission itself became a target when teenagers interfered with meetings by beating up some of the young people whom the sisters loved and by raising catcalls outside the chapel windows during worship services.[37] As they approached two decades of faithful service, Amanda and Mary gradually withdrew into a shell of fear and paranoia. They closed the windows and pulled the curtains to the street. They locked their outside gate. They warned visitors of the dangers in the neighborhood.[38]

To make matters worse, the news from home became more and more confusing. As the Eastern Board consolidated its mission efforts, John H. Mellinger and other leaders began asking whether the time had come to disband the Sunday School Mission. At the 87th quarterly meeting on July 25, 1917, the members of this lay mission movement agreed to give their work over to the Eastern Board. Four times a year for seventeen years, the sister workers had looked forward to the Sunday School Mission's public meetings, often writing letters home or reports in the church paper about renewed energy and inspiration after a day of spiritual refreshment at either the Paradise or Kinzer Mennonite meetinghouse.[39] What would Amanda Musselman and Mary Denlinger do without this consistent fountain of support?

Because they were women, Amanda and Mary had only limited access to the inner workings of the Eastern Board. Unlike the Sunday School Mission, where decisions were made at public meetings, the Eastern Board made its decisions at private executive committee meetings, reporting monthly to the Bishop Board and annually to the constituency.[40]

Although the men of the Eastern Board were discreet about recording any specific criticism or disapproval, the minutes did not conceal their growing concern with "volunteer missionaries." In March 1921, Noah H. Mack preached a pointed sermon entitled "How to Create and Maintain a Healthy Missionary Spirit." John Weaver asked for a resolution to have "an ordained man at each mission."

The resolution passed. On April 5, 1922, David Garber preached the sermon that would become the Eastern Board's unofficial motto: "Lengthening our Cords and Strengthening the Stakes." In the ensuing years, most workers came to understand that this motto meant the Eastern Board was willing to work with a long cord to distant missions as long as the workers stayed connected to the strong stakes at home.

That spring of 1922, the Bishop Board took a decisive step to strengthen the stake connecting the Philadelphia mission. Bishop C. M. Brackbill asked a young New Holland couple, J. Paul and Phebe Graybill, to move to Philadelphia.[41] Amanda, especially, struggled with this suffocating change. After working independently as they believed God had called them for twenty-three years, the sister workers felt themselves under siege. Their support network had disappeared. Their neighborhood had deteriorated. Their cherished home must now be shared with Amanda's much younger and newly married niece, Phebe Martin Graybill, and her husband Paul.

In October 1922, Phebe and J. Paul arrived to replace Amanda and Mary as the central figures of the Philadelphia

Home Mission. Young and full of fresh ideas, J. Paul, a minister, wanted to open the curtains and gates. He suggested outdoor services and summer Bible school in Norris Square Park across the street, but Amanda and Mary remained cautious and unbending. On January 30, 1923, Amanda wrote home, "Bro. Graybill is writing just now too. Phebe is in the kitchen, helping something. Possibly toward the dinner, they are getting acquainted and doing things, we are leading gently as we can."

The gentle leading disintegrated rapidly, however, and J. Paul and Phebe left the mission nine months later, in November 1923. Speaking in 1998, Ruth Myers Wyble recalled how Amanda explained the sisters' dilemma: "Amanda never wanted to talk about it, but my dad came right out and asked her what happened when she stayed with us in 1924. She said Paul told them he came to boss, not to be bossed."[42]

The uneven communication between the men of the Eastern Board and the sister workers eventually gave way to an earthquake. On April 10, 1924, in directing the actions of the Eastern Board, the Bishop Board instructed J. Paul Graybill to return to Philadelphia and take charge of the work at the mission.[43] Paul and Phebe hesitated because of "the resistance of sister Amanda Musselman who emphatically protested against the labors of brother and sister Paul Graybill at the said mission where they had been placed as workers by the Eastern board of missions and charities at the recommendation of the board of bishops," Bishop Board minutes record. The Bishop Board appointed a committee of three men "to investigate by hearing sister Musselman and report their findings to the board of bishops."[44]

The three men attempted to work out the differences, sincerely negotiating to make a place for Amanda and Mary. C. M. Brackbill, a member of the investigating committee and the bishop who originally invited J. Paul and Phebe to Philadelphia, pled for patience and tolerance toward the sisters. "There are so many good things that have been done; that covers a multitude of mistakes," he wrote.[45] Within a month of Brackbill's plea to his fellow committee members, the sisters' many years of steadfast service came to an abrupt and inglorious end.

Amanda Musselman and Mary Denlinger suddenly left Philadelphia the week of July 27, 1924. It was twenty-five summers and half a lifetime since they had cleaned and scrubbed the humble house on East York Street and greeted their first Sunday school children. Amanda was fifty-four; Mary was fifty-six. They retrieved their belongings over the next year.

J. Paul and Phebe returned to Philadelphia sometime during the turbulent week of July 27, 1924. The sisters were probably gone by the time the Graybills unloaded their belongings. Mary's final mission report to the church paper, written July 23, mentioned the impending arrival of the Graybills: "Paul and Phebe Graybill and little Naomi will have returned to Philadelphia before this letter reaches the readers." Several Kensington-area members of Amanda and Mary's mission community wrote to the investigating committee, pleading for the sisters' reinstatement. Neither Eastern Board nor the Bishop Board left any record of responses.[46]

Under J. Paul Graybill's leadership, stability returned to the Philadelphia mission. Summer Bible schools brought rural Lancastrians to the neighborhood, where they had a chance to witness life in the big city. Outdoor hymn sings and tent meetings in the park across the street attracted youth and adults. The mission became Norris Square Mennonite Church in July 1938. A number of neighborhood children who came to faith through Amanda and Mary's work were among the adult charter members of this city congregation.[47]

Amanda and Mary spent nearly two years in Mummasburg, Pennsylvania, with one of Amanda's cousins. There they attended a Mennonite church that had supported their Philadelphia work.[48] In September 1926, Amanda bought a house on East Chestnut Street in Lancaster, and Mary moved in with her. Together they ministered to the neighborhood, becoming members of the nearby East Chestnut Street Mennonite Church. Mary walked six blocks to Thaddeus Stevens Trade School, where she worked as a housekeeper, and Amanda provided room and board to a parade of young men who were students at the Lancaster school.[49] The last fourteen years of their life together mirrored the relative peace and prosperity of the first fourteen in Philadelphia.

When Amanda died June 17, 1940, in their home, Mary, along with Amanda's sister Katie, was at her side.[50] Several weeks later, Mary eulogized Amanda's life and work in *Gospel Herald*. "Her whole aim in life was to win others to Jesus and have them live fully surrendered lives, which she knew was the only way to enjoy His full blessing. . . . In the quietude of this service [the funeral], listening to the Word of God, one noticed how the trees outside were bending in the strong winds, almost to the ground, yet they came up tall and straight again. It was typical of her life. . . . The following brothers and sister survive: Eli, Amos, and Katie Myers, all of New Holland, Pa.; Sister Mary S. Denlinger and a large number of relatives and friends will also miss her inspirational life."[51]

One hundred years after Amanda and Mary arrived in Kensington, a vibrant Spanish-speaking Mennonite congregation fills the benches of 2151 North Howard Street on Sunday mornings. The Philadelphia Home Mission's incarnation, Arca de Salvación, once again functions independently under Lancaster Mennonite Conference oversight. Now an *iglésia*, the mission has come full circle. It manages its own treasury and makes its own decisions.

Sister Sauder

No complete signature could be found. Lydia was called "Sister Sauder" numerous times in the minutes of the Millersville Children's Home. This particular entry was written in the hand of Jacob D. Mellinger, the board secretary, about a year before he married her.

His WifeThen Took Charge

Lydia Stauffer Sauder Mellinger
Millersville, Pennsylvania

IN THE SUMMER OF 1892, when Lydia Stauffer was only fourteen, the Samuel and Maria Stauffer family endured a season of almost unbearable heartbreak and loss. It was a summer that transformed the world for the Stauffer children, opening young Lydia's heart to the growing revival fire of Mennonite evangelists. On June 20, 1892, her nine-year-old sister Mary succumbed to a fever of the brain. Mother Maria, who was pregnant with her tenth child, gave birth to baby Elmer on July 29, only to lose him six days later. Unable to recover from the complications of childbirth and those sad days, Maria Stauffer also died on September 12, 1892. She left behind a husband and eight children ages three to eighteen. Maria was only forty-one.[1]

Like many nineteenth-century Lancaster Mennonites, Samuel and Maria attended church, but they had never been baptized. Congregations such as Groffdale and Metzler, each only a few miles from the Stauffers' Farmersville home, tolerated a wide range of self-expression while encouraging young parents to teach their children well. In the eyes of the revival preachers, these Mennonite churches were much too complacent. In the eyes of people like Samuel and Maria Stauffer, baptism and church membership exacted a high price, requiring a stricter dress code and fewer connections to the local community. Young Mennonite parents who enjoyed the world often preferred to wait for baptism and church membership.[2]

On sensing the severity of her situation, Maria "requested to be received into church membership by water baptism, but died before this was accomplished, though she died with the living hope of meeting a reconciled God," her obituary noted.[3]

Joseph Wenger preached her funeral sermon on Romans 6:23: "For the wages of sin is death; but the gift of God is eternal life through Jesus Christ our Lord." Given the nature of Maria's death, the text was either completely comforting or wildly inappropriate, depending on which of the two phrases Joseph Wenger used to define this Mennonite mother's life.

She was laid to rest in the Metzler Mennonite Church cemetery on September 14, 1892, two months and twenty-five days after the death of her daughter Mary. Maria's obituary only hinted at the pain of losing two children and a wife and mother in the space of one summer: "She leaves her sorrowing husband and eight children to mourn her death."[4] Young Lydia, the oldest daughter, inherited the household burdens, "taking charge of the family fireside," as one family historian noted.[5]

Living near the heart of the Groffdale-Metzler Mennonite community, the Stauffer children and young people were soon attracted to and changed by the energy of the 1890s Great Awakening. Lydia was nineteen in 1898 when, as she later wrote, "the Lord called me very definitely to serve Him."[6] Young and impressionable, she immediately resolved to obey God's call and join the emerging Mennonite mission field.

"*How?*" she wrote, "was the question that was before me as it was in the days when our beloved church was not so active in mission work."[7] How would a teenager turning twenty find a place to serve in the limited (though slowly expanding) range of Lancaster Mennonite mission activity? Where would she go? What would she do? Lydia wondered, but she decided to wait for a more direct invitation from the church.

It was a time of discontent and change for the Lancaster Mennonite community. Some folks around Farmersville rejoiced in the revival movement and celebrated its emphases on witness and mission. Others questioned the movement's fiery emotionalism. Some praised its positive influences. Others considered it unnecessarily divisive. Some believed God was calling Mennonite missionaries to go "into all the world and preach the gospel." Others preferred to stay with the old ways, keeping their children close to them and living quietly in stately stone and brick houses with manicured farms, gardens, and lawns.

Lydia joined with those who supported the 1890s revival. Leaders such as Noah Mack, John Mellinger, and Samuel Musselman began tapping the shoulders of young women and men, suggesting they follow God's call to the mission field. They described Sunday school needs on the Mine Ridge above the Pequea Valley, a city mission in Philadelphia, and a possible outreach near Mount Airy on top of the Welsh Mountain, a steep, six-mile buggy ride from Farmersville. After her call, Lydia anticipated she would be invited to one of these places. She just didn't know how, when, or to which one.

Early in 1898, the year of Lydia's call, Sam Musselman and a board of twelve directors first investigated mission possibilities on the Welsh Mountain. Before that time, many residents of both the Conestoga and Upper Pequea valleys shunned the mountain because of its reputation as a haven for beggars and thieves. Writing in July 1901, a reporter for the *Reading Eagle* declared it had once been "a tangle of briars, weeds and brush, isolated as it were from mankind, where all sorts of wickedness could be carried on unknown to the outside world."[8]

The mountain people included children of former slaves as well as many Scots-Irish and Welsh immigrants. The enclave of African-Americans, seeking refuge from an unjust social and political system, had settled around the Hand Boards area on the mountain's northwestern slope. Other residents lived in scattered communities up and down the hollows and ridges. Most mountaineers maintained a hardscrabble and honest life, eking what they could from the crags, hillocks, and plateaus.

Lack of opportunity and money provoked some to criminal action, however. A notorious gang of white outlaws terrorized black mountain residents as well as white people in the valleys for nearly half a century. A sweeping crackdown in the 1880s and 1890s hauled most of them off to jail.[9] Several black men were also jailed for persistent nighttime raids to steal chickens and other livestock from valley farmers. The mountain life was a harsh life. Lydia Stauffer and most other young Mennonites stayed as far away as they could.

In January 1895, John R. Buckwalter asked an urgent question of a gathering of the Lancaster Sunday School Mission. "We see among other scenes, the beautiful Welsh Mountain, peopled with a people to our certain knowledge of both races of whom it can be truly said as the Lord said of the Ninevites, that they cannot discern between the right hand and the left. And what have we as a Church done to save them?"[10]

The answer was obvious: little. When the mountain people came down to the valleys with aging horses and broken wagons, Mennonites gave what they could but rarely socialized with the poor folks living above their farms. In general New Holland-area Mennonites did not associate with mountain people. Lydia Stauffer probably knew no one on the mountain.

As John Buckwalter and Sam Musselman campaigned to change Mennonite perceptions and bring hope to mountain folks, they met Melford Hagler, a seminary-trained Presbyterian pastor who was black. Together, these men solicited support to build the first Lancaster Mennonite self-help project, the Welsh Mountain Industrial Mission.[11]

Melford farmed a small acreage on the mountain and ministered to the Hand Boards community from a tiny stone chapel, Mt. Hope Presbyterian Church. In July 1897, he attended the quarterly mission meeting at Paradise. He spoke, convincing many that the time had come to build a mission on the mountain. Although Melford Hagler was never granted an official position on the Welsh Mountain board, his firm insistence on self-sufficiency influenced everything Mennonites accomplished among his people.[12] Maintaining a strong conviction that the mountain people needed to learn useful trades, Melford's suggestions merged smoothly with the Swiss-South German work ethic of his benefactors. On March 18, 1898, the Welsh Mountain mission board, led by Sam Musselman, arrived at Mount Airy. Twenty-two men and boys from the mountain joined the Mennonites to clear several acres of brush and small trees from a plot of land purchased by the board.[13]

A year later when local school teacher and mission enthusiast Noah H. Mack contemplated moving to the mission to supervise its budding agricultural and industrial activities, his wife Elizabeth insisted that they not go to the mountain alone. It was she who invited their neighbor, Lydia Stauffer, to join them. Some people around Farmersville raised questions about whether Lydia should go. Like her friends and neighbors, she was nervous about the location, but Lydia knew God had called her. She said yes. Her nineteen-year-old sister Julia took over the responsibilities in the Stauffer home.[14]

On April 4, 1899, Lydia climbed into Sam Musselman's carriage for the early spring trek up the mountain. Some forty years later, she remembered the stirrings in her spirit on that morning. "I believe it was as much of an adventure to go there as it is to go to Africa these days. The morning we left home the Lord spoke very definitely to my heart and gave me the message, 'Fear thou not; for I am with thee: be not dismayed; for I am thy God: I will strengthen thee: yea, I will help thee; yea, I will uphold thee with the right hand of my righteousness' [Isa. 41:10]. This was a step in faith, but who could not go forth with such a promise given. I can still hear Bro. S. H. Musselman say over and over as we climbed up the mountain with horse and carriage, 'I will go before you into Galilee.'"[15] Sam's comforting words calmed the nervous heart of Lydia Stauffer. She celebrated her twenty-first birthday on April 20, at the dawn of an illustrious career in the Lancaster Mennonite Conference.

The ten acres purchased by the industrial mission proved fertile, and the face of the plateau quickly changed. A store stocked with donated clothing and groceries opened in one room of the rather primitive house where Noah, Elizabeth, their daughter, Anna, and Lydia first lived. The land, Noah wrote to the *Herald of Truth*, would be used "for garden farming and the raising of small fruit. This kind of farming gives much work and also larger income from a small space of ground than raising of grain would from the same area."[16]

Potatoes, strawberries, and broom corn filled the fields that summer. The locals prospered; begging and stealing nearly disappeared. Lydia and Elizabeth cared for the home and store while Noah worked alongside his hired hands. In his report, Noah described an unexpected problem: "The greatest difficulty we have found yet was that when work stopped on the mission for a space of time, they [men, women, and children] begged for work until we provided them again with work."[17]

The three missionaries worried about finances while looking forward to brighter days. "This mission is now a financial burden, but if we are all faithful, supporting it and managing it, doing all our work in sincerity and with singleness of heart, it is going to bring an income to the church in the future," wrote Noah. "This we sincerely believe."[18]

Noah's regular financial reports to *Herald of Truth* were meant to inform the church of the growing financial burden. In retrospect, they raise questions about risk-taking by the Welsh Mountain board. By February 26, 1901, the board had built a stone house—luxurious by mountain standards—for Noah, Elizabeth, and Lydia "to supply a suitable and reasonably safe place of living."[19] They opened a sewing factory, broom-making operation, and carpet-weaving room. They sent more workers—Jacob H. Mellinger, Magdalena Hershey, and Lizzie Wenger—to the mountain, vastly increasing support needs.

With the possible exception of the mission home, which the mountain people called "The Big House," each early enterprise advanced the stated vision:[20] "The work of this mission in the first place is to find work for and give employment to these neglected people. There has been preaching and teaching done on the Mountain at times for years, but it seemed all to no avail, unless there be some organized effort made to give these people something to do so as to establish steady habits of industry, economy and discipline which as we have already experienced, leads to self-support and to a better state of morality."[21] Holding a classic view of self-help mission work, Noah Mack, Lydia Stauffer, and the other valley Mennonites longed to lead their mountain friends to prosperity as well as to Jesus Christ.

Lydia and the other workers settled into a farm-and-home routine. They received no pay, and their local employees, according to one observer, were also subject to the mission's concepts of simplicity and hard work. "The price paid for the work seemed very small; from twenty-five to thirty-five cents a day is earned. The men in the fields earn a dollar a day."[22]

The Welsh Mountain missionaries were typical Lancaster County Mennonites, extolling a healthy frugality tempered by occasional unexplained extravagances. These conflicting impulses supported both volunteer labor and expensive buildings, low wages and modern sewing or carpet-making equipment, fields of corn and such hard-to-grow fruits as strawberries, blackberries, and raspberries. One season the potato crop failed because of defective seed and dry weather. Several years later, that same field produced 1,200 bushels of homegrown potatoes that were taken to Lancaster city markets and sold for welcome cash.[23]

"We expect before long to have a good general store," wrote Lydia and the other sister workers in their October 1903 report to the *Herald of Truth*. Lydia took over much of the store after Noah's August 1900 Groffdale ordination. From then on he was often gone for weeks, working as a traveling evangelist. Elizabeth and Anna sometimes accompanied him.[24]

In their 1903 letter, Lydia and the other storekeepers lamented lack of freedom to purchase goods. "On account of the shortness of funds we are compelled to move slowly in this as in all other parts of the work."[25] The store became a community center where local people could purchase affordable clothing, groceries, and other necessities. The sister workers made two firm rules: no one could spit tobacco juice on the floor, and no cigars, cigarettes, or other forms of tobacco would be sold. Otherwise, everyone was welcome, regardless of race or creed.

Some mountain and valley people questioned the wisdom of encouraging friendships between the mountain residents and the missionaries, who brought with them both cultural and racial differences. Perhaps partly because of this, Melford Hagler agreed to continue providing spiritual nourishment for black mountain residents. The missionaries held private services in the Big House or traveled to their home congregations in the valleys. Noah Mack expressed discomfort with this segregation as early as fall 1899. "We have thus far not done a great deal directly towards their spiritual improvement on an organized plan. The Lord has not opened a way."[26]

In the summer of 1901, Melford asked the Sunday School Mission to support opening a Sunday school for African Americans at Mt. Hope Chapel. Ira Hershey came up from the valley to assist him. By 1903 the Welsh Mountain missionaries were opening the doors of the Big House every Tuesday night for an integrated worship service of Bible reading and prayer.[27]

During these years, Lydia taught a toddler Sunday school class at Red Well, a white Mennonite mission at the foot of the mountain. One Sunday morning she fretted over having no money for the offering. As she walked the two miles down to Red Well, she prayed, asking God to understand her constraints as an unsalaried missionary. Looking ahead, the glint of a copper penny caught her eye. She gave praise for this compelling reminder of God's providence and dropped the penny into Red Well's offering basket.

To Lydia Stauffer, God was ever-personal and ever-present. Reflecting this concept of God, she projected a loving, personal presence in her interactions with other people. Faithfulness embodied her life, and service to others brought her great satisfaction. She helped Elizabeth Mack adjust to the Welsh Mountain. She helped later workers find their places at the mission. She helped the children at Red Well. Sometime in 1903, the Welsh Mountain board asked Lydia and Magdalena Hershey to become house visitors. Regularly, they called on people up and down the mountain who did not attend either of the Sunday schools, supplying lesson papers and giving membership cards to those who were willing to study at home.[28]

One day when Noah and Elizabeth were gone, Lydia and Magdalena looked up from their work in the store to see one of the mountain's "bad characters" come through the door. Within a few minutes and to the young women's great relief, the mission's righthand man, Samuel Green, also walked in. He had observed the man's arrival and offered his assistance should the unwelcome caller create a disturbance. No harm came to anyone. But the thought of what might have happened prompted Lydia to remember, "We had many pleasant experiences and many not so pleasant."[29] It also prompted the Welsh Mountain board to seek a man to manage and mind the store.

In what proved a life-altering event for Lydia Stauffer, they found Levi Sauder. He was Noah Mack's nephew, an apprenticed storekeeper, and a widower accustomed to mountain living. As a teenager, Levi had trained in several country stores near his home in Bowmansville.[30] He married Mollie Snyder in 1901 and moved to Roaring Spring, a village at the southern end of Morrison's Cove in Pennsylvania's ruggedly beautiful Blair County. Mollie died only a week after the birth of their first child, and Levi dedicated himself to caring for their son, often writing short reports about the Mennonite congregation at Roaring Spring for the *Herald of Truth*.

Early in 1906, Levi and his four-year-old son, J. Paul, arrived on the Welsh Mountain. No letters or records of a courtship have surfaced, but Lydia Stauffer quickly accepted this man who came to take over what was essentially her store. Levi was an easygoing, gentle man, and he did not push her out. Instead, the two became partners. On August 23, 1906, they were married.

Four years later when Noah and Elizabeth Mack left the mountain work, Levi and Lydia Sauder agreed to become resident superintendent and matron. Around this time the Sauders became aware of a budding new mission opportunity. Lancaster County Mennonites were advocating the formation of a children's home "to be a centre for gathering homeless children, who will be sent out from that place to permanent homes in good families," according to one newspaper announcement.[31]

A board of trustees, led by John H. Mellinger, assigned a site committee, purchased land near the Lancaster-Millserville trolley line, and solicited funds to construct a three-story, red-brick building. People as different in mission orientation as Lancaster Conference Mennonites around Weaverland and Amish Mennonites of Conestoga and Millwood joined the cause. Money flowed in. Labor and materials followed. This unusual marriage of Mennonite and Amish-Mennonite neighbors furnished broad support for the children's home that was noticed by the trustees. Article IV of the bylaws decreed "two members of the Board shall be of the Amish Mennonite brethren."[32]

From their mountain home, Levi and Lydia contemplated the new ministry and its supporters. They soon made a decision. On New Year's Day 1911, Levi approached John Mellinger at the East Chestnut Street meetinghouse and said, "My wife and I have a conviction for entering children's home work." John responded, "That's what I wanted to say to you. Will you be the superintendent and matron of the Children's Home?"[33]

Levi, Lydia, and eight-year-old J. Paul moved from the Welsh Mountain about forty miles southwest to the Millersville Children's Home on March 22, 1911. Lydia had lived on the mountain a few weeks shy of twelve years. She had arrived as an eager but inexperienced novice and left as a seasoned missionary leader with responsibilities for a home, husband, and school-age son. The Sauders were entering an uncharted sea, a new work where Lydia and Levi would affectionately be called Mama and Papa Sauder by hundreds of needy children.

A week after the Sauders came to Millersville, Mary Denlinger walked up to the front door with four children she and Amanda Musselman had befriended at the Philadelphia Home Mission. The Rodgers family—nine-month-old Laura, three-year-old Bertha, five-year-old Gertrude, and eight-year-old Walter—posed for a photograph on the front steps of the Children's Home. Their innocent faces held oceans of pain.[34]

Nine months after the Rodgers children arrived, Mama and Papa Sauder had sixteen children in their charge. In keeping with their mandate to place "such as are advisable in private homes," they had also shepherded another sixteen youngsters into foster homes.[35]

Photographs of Lydia and Levi at the Home usually show them side-by-side with arms touching, though never obviously holding hands. In one a rosebush blooms behind where they stand, Lydia beaming at an elegantly dressed girl in Levi's arms. In another they sit close together on a plush sofa, pleasant smiles and soft eyes directed to the camera.

Mama and Papa Sauder worked hard, supervising the children and a staff of young Mennonite women. A typical Children's Home day started at 6:00 a.m. as the housemothers awakened the youngsters while the cooks started breakfast. After the children were washed and dressed, they scampered from their second-floor rooms to the first-floor kitchen for breakfast. Levi then gathered everyone in the sun parlor for a half-hour of worship. Next came chores for the older children—emptying trash, sweeping walks, and feeding pets. In the winter, the school-age children made their way to the Model School of a local teacher's college, the Millersville State Normal School.[36] In the summer, they played or worked in the garden and lawn.

At 5:00 p.m. supper was served. During mild weather, the children and caregivers might spend evenings turning homemade ice cream or feasting on homegrown watermelons. When winter came, quiet times of reading or playing filled the twilight hours. The housemothers initiated bedtime at 7:00 p.m., ushering the children to large rooms lined with single cots.

With the concern and tenderness modeled by Mama and Papa Sauder, the caregivers did their best to alleviate the stress of nighttime in an orphanage. They stayed with the children, praying, playing games, or reading books as the youngsters slowly settled into sleep. After choosing a record for the Victrola, housemothers typically left the bedrooms by 8:00 p.m.[37]

The Children's Home had its problems. Sometimes the children thought Mama and Papa Sauder too strict.[38] Their strong streak of personal piety was foreign to many of the children. As a younger man, Levi had penned a Christmas article for the church paper entitled "Santa Claus." He wrote, "It is thought by at least five-sixths of our innocent children that there is a human being called 'Santa Claus,' and that he makes his appearance on Christmas." This is a misrepresentation and is not substantiated with God's word. These things belong to the world. Let the world have them."[39]

Although Lydia and Levi both had missionary passion, Lydia's softer nature complimented and smoothed some of Levi's spiritual fervor, making the Children's Home a nurturing and safe place for most of the children. Through the years, the children came back to Mama and Papa Sauder for advice and counsel in raising their own families. Many grew up and became successful, well-adjusted adults who spoke of their surrogate parents with admiration and respect. "I loved Mama and Papa Sauder. They were wonderful to me," says one. "I appreciated Levi Sauder. He was strict but fair," says another. "Mama and Papa Sauder had an outstanding relationship with children. They could meet and fill their needs," yet another recounts.[40]

In fall 1912, thirty-five-year-old Lydia became pregnant. Levi and Lydia's son John Levi was born June 13, 1913. No records survive to illuminate how this may have changed the Children's Home climate. John's older half-brother, J. Paul, was almost eleven. Lydia continued as matron while overseeing care of her two boys. As they had from the day the Home opened, the Sauder family shared living space, meals, and time with the children and sister workers. A foster son, Richard, joined the active, crowded household November 1919. Though she now had three growing sons, Lydia evidently skipped few beats in her Children's Home-related responsibilities.

Children came to the Sauders for many reasons. Both parents had died, their mothers were unwed teenagers, or their families had disintegrated because of abuse, crime, or poverty. The Home also opened its doors to parents who were temporarily unable to care for their children because of some unexpected tragedy—an accident, a fire, the loss of a job. These parents generally paid a small support fee. The year of John Levi's birth, one such father forcibly removed his daughter from the Home. Angry about the fee, he threatened to kill Levi if he followed him out the door. Levi did not follow.[41]

Five years later, the devastating 1918 influenza epidemic swept across Lancaster County. Most of the children and workers fell ill, and the Home was placed under quarantine by the city board of health.[42] One of the Rodgers children, the first set to arrive at the Home, died. The local doctor died. Like most victims of the 1918 epidemic, they were buried without funerals. Too ill to attend the burials, Levi asked Lydia to prop him up in bed where he could see the Millersville Mennonite cemetery and watch as their friends and neighbors were laid to rest. Lydia worked day and night nursing the sick.[43]

The state health department urged people to abide by the quarantines, avoid crowds and stress, eat a variety of foods, and get as much fresh air as possible. They also suggested a preventive measure—fill a nasal dropper with a solution including iodine and take it a few times daily.[44] Thanks in large part to Mama Sauder's tireless efforts, Levi and most of the Home's children and workers took a turn for the better and survived.

Levi and Lydia immediately renewed their earlier request for another building, listing four reasons why they needed this additional house: in case of epidemics, for segregation of boys and girls, to separate the older children from the babies, and to give more space for winning souls. But the Mennonites and Amish of 1919 proved much less generous than they had been in 1909. Lydia Stauffer no doubt remembered the debt an early building project brought to the Welsh Mountain work. Although it took another ten years, the Sauders and their board waited to break ground until they had the money in hand.

Lydia and Levi were a superb management team. More frugal than the Welsh Mountain workers had been, they apparently never carried a debt while supplying the needs of the Home's children and workers, as well as their own family, for thirty years. The centerpiece of their frugality was the Home's huge garden and an adjacent orchard. Together they planted, raised, and preserved much of their own food.

Lydia managed the workers, overseeing day-to-day domestic operations. Levi managed the finances, maintaining a fine rapport with the local Mennonite constituency.[45] The community responded with a consistent outpouring of gifts and services. Sewing circles delivered new outfits for the children. Volunteer laborers mended clothing, cleaned the Home's facilities, and helped with garden work. Each spring Levi delivered hundreds of empty canning jars to Mennonite congregations across Lancaster County. By fall the Home's vast cellar sparkled with colorful jars of beef, chicken, corn, peas, beans, and many varieties of fruit or pickled vegetables.[46]

Then on March 22, 1927, two armed men stormed into the house, finding Lydia, Levi, and seven-year-old Richard, the foster son they had recently adopted. "After I was adopted, I could stay up later than the other children," recalls Richard. "We were sitting in the living room when these two guys busted in. They put the gun to Papa's head. One grabbed Mama and threw her against the wall. I went crazy. They kept asking for

Laura. One stood guard while the other forced me to go with him upstairs. He was looking for Laura Mae Miller.

"While Laura was a child," Richard explains, "her mother didn't want her. But once Laura turned sixteen, the mother decided she should come home, get a job, and give her whatever money Laura could earn. That mother hired those two men to kidnap Laura."[47]

As the appointed sentry trained a gun at Levi's head, Levi looked him in the eye and said, "Young man, if you shoot me down, I will pray for your forgiveness with my last breath."

The other bandit propelled Laura Mae down the steps where she encountered the Sauders and their guard. Running to Levi, she cried, "Papa! Please help me." The puzzled would-be kidnappers asked, "Aren't you coming with us?" When she adamantly refused, they backed out the front door, guns still aimed at the terrified quartet, and ran into the night.

Within hours, local authorities apprehended the hapless criminals, along with Laura Mae's mother. One gunman later testified, "When that preacher said that he would pray for me even if I shot him, I couldn't do anything to him."[48]

After that frightening evening, life at the Home became more stable. The administration building finally opened in early 1929. Lydia and Levi had their much-longed-for infirmary. For the first time in twenty-two years of marriage, they also had their own living space. J. Paul was married, and that same year his wife Alice gave birth to Levi and Lydia's first grandchildren, twin boys named Joseph Paul and John Allan. John Levi turned sixteen in June. Richard celebrated his tenth birthday a few days after the October stock market crash. His concerns were more personal: "After we moved over to the superintendent's house, John and I each got our own bedrooms."

Eleven years later, Lydia's longtime companion collapsed while leading the Home's children through morning devotions.

Levi died October 28, 1940. A glimpse into the character of Lydia Sauder can be found in five simple words written in the records of the Children's Home: "His wife then took charge."[49]

Not a woman easily recognized for her church leadership gifts, Lydia gave her entire life to the work of the church. She was a different kind of leader. After managing the Children's Home through winter, spring, and summer, she turned the work over to her sister Julia and her husband, Gideon Eberly. Lydia's three sons were married. Her many other children were in good hands. It was time for Mama Sauder to move on.

On December 14, 1941, Lydia married Jacob D. Mellinger, a Rohrerstown truck farmer seven years younger. He had served on the Children's Home board and lost his own companion soon after Levi died. In February 1942, Jacob and Lydia took over as camp directors at the World War II Civilian Public Service (CPS) barracks near Hagerstown, Maryland. Lydia had a new title: Mom Mellinger. In 1946 as the war ended and the camps prepared to close, Mom and Pop Mellinger left Camp #24. Later the same day, they pulled into the parking lot of Mennonite Old People's Home at Oreville (now Mennonite Home in Lancaster) as its new steward and matron.[50]

In her final ministry among the aging, Lydia extended the same commitment that she had given to all phases of her work. Her lifelong service to the church brought blessing and hope to thousands of people for more than fifty years. Except for the four years in Maryland, all of her service took place in Lancaster County, with the people among whom she was born and raised.

Lydia Mellinger died on June 27, 1952, during a severe midsummer heat wave. She was supervising cherry canning in the kitchen of the Mennonite Home.[51] After her death, husband Jacob wrote, "I cannot find words to describe this saintly mother, friend, and most of all a faithful, loving, sincere, and devoted wife."[52]

Phebe Yoder

3

A Planter of Trees

Phebe Ethel Yoder
Mugango and Bukiroba, Tanzania

On a winter evening in 1912, nine-year-old Phebe Yoder hiked the half mile along a Kansas country road to West Liberty Mennonite Church. With her parents, Charles and Susanna Heatwole Yoder, and her siblings, Phebe was going to a revival service led by Lancaster County evangelist Noah H. Mack. As was his custom, Noah preached a pulpit-pounding sermon before offering an altar call. That evening young Phebe, born January 26, 1903, committed her life to Christ.[1] Through her remaining days, she remembered that McPherson County church, the Pennsylvania preacher, and the winter night with this simple phrase: "I was converted when I was nine years old."[2]

Phebe's parents were farmers. The Yoder homestead, with its three-story house filled with children and its small red barn with farm animals, nurtured both fun and faithfulness. "I come from a family of ten children, five brothers and four sisters. And we had one big time in our life. Even today I believe in having a good time," Phebe told friends later in life. As eldest daughter and second-oldest child, she coordinated ball games, skating parties, and other family activities. "I had a lot of pep."

She also loved to read. Sophia Lyon Fahs's biography of the life of Alexander Mackay, *Uganda's White Man of Work,* so impressed the twelve-year-old Phebe that she knelt beside her bed after closing its pages and promised one day to go to Africa. From that time forward, she set her mind on doing just that. Many Sunday afternoons found her alone in the Yoder barn's granary, Sunday school papers tacked to a wall. There she stood before an imaginary class of African children, teaching the word of God. "Of course, I didn't stop to think that I couldn't teach them in English," she recalled later. "I didn't know about Swahili back then." In those quiet moments, the only voice that mattered was the voice of God—a voice that allowed a Mennonite prairie girl to dream of leaving her small Kansas world for a life-changing experience on another continent.

For many years, Phebe kept the call to herself.[3] "The time between when you're twelve years old and the time when you're sent is a long time and lots of things happen." Although mission fields and recruiting workers were front-burner topics in the 1920s Mennonite community, there was no work in Africa. Neither was it considered appropriate, especially for women, to put themselves forward, to announce a call, or to volunteer for service.

Mennonites of the 1920s and 1930s waited to be asked. This philosophy so permeated the churchwide Mennonite mission movement that most people rarely, if ever, spoke on their own behalf. Few had the audacity to say, "I would like to go," or "I am called." Instead, they prayed and waited until mission leaders such as Henry Garber and Orie Miller issued personal invitations to a particular work.

As Phebe waited, she worked at other pursuits. She attended the nearby Mennonite high school in Hesston, taught several years to save money for more education, went back to Hesston for college-level classes, and taught school again.

While teaching near her McPherson County home during one of the seasons of saving for higher education, she fell in love. "His name was George, a fine Christian man, the Sunday school superintendent of our church there," Phebe recalled later. She was twenty-one when George turned to her and asked, "Can you marry me? Can we get married?" There in the grasslands of central Kansas, Phebe Yoder's pulse picked up and her heart fluttered as she said yes.

Within minutes, though, her pulse steadied as her heart yielded to reason. For the first time, she shared the story of her childhood promise to God. "Do you also hear a call to go to Africa?" she asked George. For her, the summons to Africa was as clear as it had been the night she finished reading the account of Alexander Mackay's work in Uganda.

It was not so for George. "I don't feel that God wants us to go to Africa. Don't you know there are many people here in America who need to hear the gospel?" he replied.

But there was no convincing Phebe. She reversed her earlier yes and said no to George. "I shed some tears," she told friends later. "It costs tears, you know. I went back to college and our friendship broke up."

Moving forward, Phebe set her sights more firmly on the ultimate goal—a home in Africa. She often asked herself how it would happen, what she could do to help open the door, and whether it even made sense. Although she sometimes questioned her sanity, Phebe never stopped believing that the door to Africa would open. As a young adult, she even began sending her tithes to the General Mission Board (now called Mennonite Board of Missions) in Elkhart, Indiana, earmarked "for mission work in Africa."[4]

The year she turned twenty-nine, Phebe Yoder finally had enough money to enroll at Goshen College in Indiana. She packed her bags and left the big white house on the road straight west of Elyria, halfway between Inman and Windom.[5] Her father had died nine years earlier. Many of her siblings were getting married. Her new brother-in-law, Phares Loucks, and younger sister Leah took over the farm. It seemed a good time to leave.

In keeping with her "God wants us to enjoy life" philosophy, Phebe poured considerable energy into this new quest. "I lived in the dormitory. I loved every day of college. If there was anything, I was in it. I was on the basketball team. If we had a big skating party, I was there." An upfront and physically capable woman with a significant portion of her pioneer ancestors' courage and stamina, Phebe Yoder knew what she wanted to do with her life. The restrained and simple ways of her Mennonite forebears and parents reined in some of the pioneering spirit. She dressed plain. She worked hard, served the church, and prayed often.[6] And, according to one of her friends, "she was a woman who knew how to repent."[7]

At Goshen she met and began corresponding with another young man. He visited her during the Easter holiday in 1934. "Then the same word came up again," recalled Phebe. "The same word! I can remember where we sat in that reception room in that college. In my senior year. And I said the same thing." She turned to the young man (whom she never identified to anyone else, not even to her closest friends) and announced, "Well, I'm called to Africa, and I must go." They stayed in touch, but the relationship fell apart when it became obvious that he had no call to Africa.[8]

Phebe graduated from Goshen later that spring and went to New York, where she worked as nanny and tutor. While she was sitting with the children at the family's summer home on Long Island, she sorted out her future plans.[9] She learned that the General Mission Board in Elkhart had forwarded her Africa seed money to the Eastern Board in Lancaster County. They had already used the money, along with other donations, to send four workers to a developing mission opportunity in Tanganyika, a small British colony in eastern Africa (now Tanzania).

"And then the devil hounded me as he had never hounded me before," Phebe recalled later. "The devil said, 'Now you'll never go to Africa. The Lancaster board will never know any Kansas girl, and they wouldn't send you if they did!'"

What should she do? Had she been foolish to turn down two good offers of marriage? What openings would there be for single women teachers? As she prayed and wondered, an idea came to her. The mission stations would surely need nurses. "I battled it, because I didn't think I could be as successful in nursing as I was as a teacher." But as the summer progressed, she slowly adjusted to the idea.

Before the first hint of autumn colored Long Island, Phebe had taken a train back out west to the LaJunta Mennonite School of Nursing in Colorado. When she walked through the gates of the school, she wondered whether common sense had taken its leave. "I asked, 'Why am I locking myself into this place?'"

Then in 1937 a steady flow of answered prayers transformed Phebe's life, rescuing her from the doubts about her calling. She was in the final semester of nurses' training, filling a required internship at a university hospital in Denver. Sometime in February, she walked into the mailroom. "Here was a letter from Allen Erb, head of nurses' training in LaJunta. He wrote, 'You have been chosen to teach in our school here in LaJunta. Could you accept this? Please let us know as soon as possible.'"

The air in the Colorado hospital seemed even thinner than normal. What was going on? How would a teaching position in the Rocky Mountains satisfy her desire to live in Africa? That evening she fell to her knees, praying and weeping in the solitude of her private dorm room. A voice reassured her, "Write to

Brother Erb and tell him you won't be able to answer for at least three weeks." She wrote and mailed the letter. Returning to her room, she enjoyed a night of peaceful rest.

The next week Phebe pulled a long, narrow envelope from her mailbox. "In those days we didn't get very many long envelopes," remembered Phebe. "But there it was, marked 'air mail,' and up in the corner 'O. O. Miller, Executive Secretary, Eastern Mennonite Board of Missions and Charities.'" Once again, the air felt light. She was breathless with excitement. "Here it is. Don't open it, but here it is!" Twenty-two years had passed since the night she sensed God's call to Africa in her bedroom in Kansas. And wonder of wonders, the Eastern Board needed a nurse.

"The mission in Africa has been looking for a nurse, mature in years and Christian experience," Phebe recited from memory, years later. "For nine months, we've been looking for one. Do you have any convictions for Africa, and would you be willing to go out under the Eastern Board?"[10]

The answers were obvious. Allen Erb received a politely worded "no." The LaJunta graduation and passing the requisite state boards provided Phebe with the Eastern Board's desired nursing credentials. The summer in Kansas prepared her family. In early September, she caught an eastbound train in Inman, disembarking half a continent from her home at the grand station house in Lancaster, Pennsylvania. It was Phebe Yoder's first visit to this hotbed of Mennonite experience and history.

A friend from her days at Hesston Academy stood on the platform as the train steamed into the station. "Margaret Horst met me at the train, carrying a covering with black strings and a package of black stockings." Years later when she told the story to several friends, Phebe and her companions roared with laughter at the image and memory. They could laugh because the rigid codes of dress no longer mattered as much to Lancaster

Conference Mennonites. But upon regaining her composure, Phebe respectfully explained, "See, she too was a western girl. And she did this out of kindness to me."

Margaret Horst knew how important black stockings and coverings with black strings were to the leaders of the Eastern Board. She urged Phebe to wear both as she made her pre-appointment visits to various Lancaster churches. The sincere 1937 missionary found it easy to comply with the expectations of the community whose blessings and financial support converted her life's calling into vibrant reality. She gladly complied.

By December of the pivotal year 1937, the reality had become vibrant indeed. Her journey was fascinating, but long. She took an ocean liner from New York to Southampton, another ship through the Mediterranean Sea, the Red Sea, and the Indian Ocean to Mombasa, Kenya. From Mombasa she boarded a train for the ride along the northern edge of the mountains of Kilimanjaro, through the hills and plains to Nairobi, and around the southern fringe of the Kenyan highlands into Kisumu, a port on Lake Victoria, where she caught a lake steamer south to Musoma, Tanganyika. At long last, Phebe Yoder had come to Africa, to a very particular piece of African soil—the Mennonite mission compound nestled between two mountains about a half mile from Mugango Bay.

The 1938 Mugango compound consisted of three main buildings—a garage for the mission pickup, a spacious two-bedroom house for Elam and Elizabeth Stauffer, and a one-room storage structure that Phebe made her own. Ever the organizer, she soon opened a clinic in the garage, arranging her medicines and supplies on the pickup's fenders. From a small table, she diagnosed ailments, dispensed medication, and offered healing advice through the cool hours of the morning. In the afternoon, she taught school, struggling at first with Swahili but soon becoming quite fluent.[11]

After the first Eastern Board deputation visited East Africa in summer 1938, Phebe learned more about the events leading up to the Africa invitation. The three-person delegation—Bishop Henry Lutz, Eastern Board president Henry Garber, and his wife Ada—brought Elam Stauffer, superintendent of the Tanganyika mission, copies of the Eastern Board minutes from 1934-1938 that related to the Africa work.

Elam had already come to respect the strength of character and purpose of mind in this woman who would become a long-time mission partner. He asked Phebe if she would like to read the minutes dealing with the mission board's search "for a nurse mature in years and Christian experience." She assented.

Phebe discovered that the British colonial government had approached Elam and other mission leaders about finding an English-speaking Mennonite nurse for its hospital in Musoma. Musoma was the center of business and commerce for the four outlying Mennonite mission stations—Bukiroba on an elevation a few miles from the port town, Shirati to the north along the lake, Bumangi in the hills to the east, and Mugango south along the lakeshore. The request was forwarded to Lancaster.

It took Orie Miller nine months to find Phebe. When he finally had her affirmative response, he sent her a letter via air mail to ask, "Could you be ready to leave in a month?" Decisive and determined as ever, Phebe informed him there was no way she would be ready that soon. "I wasn't even an R.N. yet!" she recalled. "I had to finish school. I had to say good-bye to my family. So you see, by the time I got to Musoma in December 1937, it was fifteen months later and the British already had their nurse. Did I ever thank God! I was not called to go to Africa to work with white miners and government officials. Why, that would have broken my heart all over again!"

The needs around Mugango fit much more naturally with Phebe Yoder's calling and her gifts. For her, personal faith was as easy a topic of conversation as relatives, politics, and the weather. She freely shared the story of Jesus and salvation with her neighbors, patients, and students.

She loved people. "'The more the merrier' was Phebe's motto, and crowds stimulated her. She felt at home with everyone—old people, babies, students, teachers, church elders," wrote her friend, Grace Stauffer, for an article in an Eastern Board publication.[12] After gaining a relatively solid grasp of Swahili, Phebe set out to master the local languages. She wanted to be able to share more intimately with her African friends and confidants.

Phebe also loved to plant. The hardiness of Kansas pioneers followed her to Tanganyika. Everywhere she went, she planted flowers, trees, and vegetables. Lemon, orange, mango, guava, and papaya trees soon sprouted on the Mennonite mission compounds around Lake Victoria. Sharing her seedlings with the mission's Tanganyikan neighbors as well, Phebe freely bestowed advice on plant conditions and watering needs.

In the ensuing years, Phebe's trees have grown strong and tall, spreading their branches into many conversations about Mennonite missionaries in Tanganyika. Former missionary Mahlon Hess describes his first visit to Mugango in November 1945: "We were admiring the ironwood and jacaranda trees that lined the driveways. Phebe said, 'I want you to know that for each tree you see, nineteen died.' To get them started in an area that had long dry spells each year, the trees needed regular watering. The other missionaries always gave credit to Phebe for keeping the trees alive."[13]

The trees appeared in Miriam Wenger's memories of one of her earliest driving lessons in the Mugango mission pickup. Another single worker who occasionally lived with Phebe in Mugango, Rhoda Wenger, had volunteered to teach her good friend Miriam how to drive. Rhoda explained the delicate maneuverings of gearshifts and clutches, and off the two women lurched. Suddenly Phebe burst out of her house, yelling, "Rhoda, get her to stop! She's driving over my trees!" Miriam stopped.[14]

In the photo diary of her 1988 visit to her former home in Tanzania, Catharine Leatherman saved Kodak images of full-grown trees, noting that the Daniel and Rhoda Mtoka family now owned what had been Phebe's house and garden where "Phebe's trees yielded their abundant fruits."[15]

Following Ray and Miriam Wenger's arrival in May 1938, Phebe and the younger couple became fast friends. Each morning around eleven, the Mugango workers gathered for a time of Bible study and prayer. As the days became years, Phebe's primary struggles revolved around her inner tensions between nursing and teaching. She also contracted a low-grade fever that she couldn't seem to shake.[16] Although the other workers sometimes worried about her health, Phebe forged ahead.

In late 1940, she spent some time studying languages on Ukerewe Island near Mwanza, a town in southern Tanganyika.[17] While staying with Africa Inland Mission (AIM) workers, Phebe heard Rebeka Makuru preach for the first time. This amazing woman could neither read nor write, but she could cut through all the strangeness her people felt about Christianity and explain its basic precepts in a language Tanganyikan villagers accepted and understood. Phebe went back to Mugango, where she urged Ray and Miriam to invite Rebeka to come up and "do women's work" in Jita-land.

Occasionally over the next several years, as much of the rest of the world became embroiled in World War II, Rebeka and Phebe traversed the Mugango-Majita area on foot, preaching to and teaching the women in small villages in the district. "Rebeka was the preacher," recalls Miriam Wenger Shenk. "Phebe sustained her with prayer and moral support."[18]

One morning Ray Wenger reported to his colleagues that Ezekiel Muganda, a Mennonite believer, objected to Rebeka's work because she could not read or write and because she was a woman. Ray suspected the young man planned to follow the women to Jita-land, determined to disturb their ministry. He prayed that Ezekiel would not follow them. Rebeka and Phebe suspected the same thing, but they prayed that he would come. He did, and Rebeka confronted him about his attitude. Ezekiel Muganda repented. His release became a shining witness of God's work, and some years later the Mugango-Majita church district ordained Ezekiel to be one of the first two native Tanganyikan pastors.[19]

Rebeka and Phebe's work among the women came near the dawn of a far-reaching work of God's grace that would be called the East Africa Revival. Those who served with Phebe when the changes began affecting the Tanganyika Mennonite mission agreed that the movement spread east across Lake Victoria from Rwanda and Uganda. In both of those countries, AIM workers responded to the Holy Spirit and repented of their superior attitudes toward Africans.[20] Their testimonies, shared in concert with African brothers and sisters, inspired Elam and Elizabeth Stauffer when they attended an AIM conference in July 1941.[21] At the urging of both Elam and Phebe, workers on the four stations around Musoma began praying for God's spirit to touch their lives.

Revival eventually swept the entire region from Lake Victoria to the Serengeti plain. Africans became Christians; North American missionaries turned from their colonial impulses and "holier than thou" attitudes. In August 1942, a weekend conference at Shirati brought the missionaries and Africans together when Elam Stauffer felt led to stop preaching and a subsequent prayer meeting dissolved into urgent weeping. The passions of the African villagers' hearts touched the more controlled emotions of the Swiss-South German missionaries in their midst. People joined each other in seeking forgiveness and healing. The word of God had come to East Africa, but in a way most Mennonite mission workers hadn't expected; they found themselves as changed as the people to whom they ministered.[22]

The mission board in Lancaster County, separated from the field when transatlantic travel became treacherous during the war, began to ask questions. Elam Stauffer and others wrote numerous letters home describing the revival and explaining why the mission workers welcomed this work of God: it was redefining the Tanganyika mission. The Eastern Board worried that "in the fervency of their new experience the missionaries would eventually form a group separate from Lancaster Conference," says one former member of the board.[23] A few Lancaster County leaders doubted the revival's validity, but the seeds had germinated. Strong trees of African leadership—both male and female—were already reaching for the sun.

Phebe moved easily from her natural way of sharing Jesus with Africans to encouraging her fellow missionaries to open their own hearts to God. When Catharine Leatherman asked Phebe how she could find this new aliveness in Christ, Phebe answered, "I can only give you my own testimony. I felt just like you. I prayed, 'Lord, show me how I am in your sight.' What he showed me was dreadful, but now I know I'm joined to Jesus."[24]

In November 1942 the mission doctor and Phebe's fellow workers finally persuaded her to take an extended health furlough in Capetown, South Africa.[25] On her way south through central Africa, Phebe lost her reading glasses. Although she prayed every day that God would help her find them again, she also slowly surrendered herself to rest, relaxing in the warm ocean breezes of this bustling South Atlantic city.

After long hours of meditation and prayer, Phebe's body, soul, and spirit were revived. She returned to Mugango and the challenging tasks of learning the local languages and helping with various building projects. When the mission proposed a single workers' house on the Mugango compound, she offered to help with the construction.

One day she took it upon herself to crawl into the attic. Soon a carpenter came racing across the grounds to Ray and Miriam Wenger's house, shouting, "Mama Wenger, Miss Yoder fell through the ceiling!" Anxiously, Miriam followed him to the site. Once inside, she discovered Phebe unhurt but mightily upset with herself. Relieved to find no broken bones and no emergency, Miriam pointed at the ceiling with its gaping hole and surrendered to a spasm of uncontrollable laughter. Phebe could not see the humor, Miriam recounts. "She was not pleased with me. I did get her to laugh about it later, though."[26]

On August 26, 1944, Phebe joined John and Catharine Leatherman and their four small children as they left Tanganyika, bound for the United States. These three workers had been next in line for home leave when the war broke out, and the Eastern Board went to extraordinary lengths to secure passage on a neutral ship from Capetown to Buenos Aires.[27] Phebe spent most of the furlough with family and friends in Kansas, far from the difficult questions the Leathermans and other workers faced in their Lancaster County homes. Had the Tanganyika Mennonite Mission failed in its duty to the home church? What was this strange revival all about? Would the missionaries abandon the Mennonite way?

Phebe's outsider status afforded her distance from the inner workings of the Lancaster Mennonite world. Furthermore, she had work to do and stories to tell. In her captivating voice, she illustrated how simple faith changed circumstances by telling various groups of people the story of her lost eyeglasses.

Each day in Capetown, Phebe told her audiences, God had prompted her to pray that the glasses would be found. On her way home to Mugango, she passed through a train station somewhere in southern Africa. The station master came running out of the ticket office. "Where is Phebe Yoder?" he called as he moved down the platform, holding up the treasured glasses. He had been checking passenger lists, hoping the woman whose name was on the case would pass through the area again. "With tears of joy, Phebe remembered her prayer and was again assured that the Lord who cared about her glasses would also fulfill his promises for the salvation of those for whom she prayed," wrote her colleague Clyde Shenk. Phebe returned to Tanganyika in July 1946.[28]

The late 1940s and 1950s were blessed years for Phebe Yoder. Elam Stauffer and the other women and men of the Tanganyika Mennonite community understood that Phebe's gifts and strengths lay in administration and teaching rather than nursing. They sought her advice. They paid attention to her suggestions. They trusted her eye for design, changing the blueprint for the teachers' houses at the Bukiroba Bible School when Phebe drew plans demonstrating how the space could be used more efficiently. Because she seldom hesitated to speak her opinion and often campaigned to swing others to her point of view, Phebe was not always easy to work with. Elam once asked another leader, "Do you ever feel we are too democratic?"[29] The two men decided to consider each issue on its own merits.

In 1947 the mission released Phebe from her nursing responsibilities and invited her to work with the government as the first education secretary for the North Mara and Musoma districts. Her work involved securing the British colonial government's permission to build schools. Once permission was granted, Phebe and the succession of young men she hired to help her could be seen bouncing along the dirt roads north and south of the Mara River. Phebe consulted with local chiefs and sub-chiefs. She walked beside them as they marked out small parcels of land on outskirts of their family villages. She designed the simple schoolhouses and sweated through the hard work of making mud bricks. "Many a time, I'd see her coming home, her legs covered with mud," remembers Miriam Wenger.[30]

One day in 1948, Phebe strode into the second-floor office of a district commissioner. She told him how attractive the government primary school buildings were. She especially liked the arched window openings, she said. Could she borrow the forms for making such windows? Of course, he told her. Phebe walked to the window, gave a hand signal to her helpers below, and thanking the commissioner, hurried down the steps. From his office, the commissioner could see the nearby government supply depot. He watched with some amusement as his employees immediately began helping Phebe's assistant load the forms. Emerging from the building as they finished, Phebe hopped into the driver's seat. Off they went to build the first Mennonite primary school in Majita.[31]

After the schools were built, it was also the education secretary's duty to order supplies, recruit African teachers, and supervise the ongoing classroom work. Mahlon Hess, who succeeded Phebe in 1953, recalls, "It was not easy work."[32]

During her second leave in the United States in 1951, Phebe renewed her friendship with George. His wife had died, and once again they discussed marriage. Unfortunately, they were as far apart as they had been in their early twenties. George wanted to spend the rest of his life in the United States. Phebe wanted to spend the rest of hers in Africa. Instead of getting married, Phebe focused her mind on fulfilling another one of her dreams. She wanted easier access to privacy in her safaris around the countryside. Why not buy a personal vehicle and have it shipped to Tanganyika?

In conversation with several of her brothers, Phebe designed a compact mobile home to fit on a Chevy truck chassis.

With their help, she built a compartment with sufficient room for a bed, her belongings, and a supply of books. On its front she painted "Baraka," (which means *blessing* in Swahili); on the side, "Abarikiwe ajae kwa jina la bwana Yesu" (*Blessed is the one who comes in the name of the Lord*); and above the rear door, the words "Duka la vitabu" (*A store of books*). She drove the top-heavy clunker from her family's farm in Kansas to the harbor in New York, where it was loaded on a ship bound for East Africa.

Through the 1950s and 1960s, "Baraka," as Phebe called the truck, was her home away from home. Translating the Bible, teaching literacy classes, and selling gospel literature were her new passions. Widely respected for her proficiency with local languages, Phebe wrote grade-school primers for the Jita, Zanaki, and Kurya people. She worked as a consultant to the main Jita language translator, creating both a Bible and hymnal for the people of Jita-land. Ever an able and quick study, Phebe Yoder was always ready to tackle a new assignment or challenge.

In December 1961, the British colonial government left Tanganyika and restored governing authority to an independent Tanzania. The new president, Julius Nyerere, decreed that everyone must learn Swahili and launched a literacy campaign. Phebe organized the "Each one, teach one" literacy program for the Musoma District, leading a class herself and sending her students back to their communities with instructions to help their families adjust to Tanzania's new national language. At each turn in the road of her missionary life, Phebe continued, with uncommon diligence, to share and teach her faith.

Back in 1945 while Phebe and the Leathermans were on their first extended home leave, Miriam Wenger's husband, Ray, had contracted malaria and died. Following Ray's death and her own furlough, Miriam returned to Mugango, where she raised three children and where she and Phebe developed an abiding friendship that grew stronger as the years passed. When Miriam's children reached high school age in the early 1960s, she made the difficult decision to move with them back to Lancaster County. Then in 1966 the Eastern Board invited Miriam to return to Tanganyika to live with Phebe at her home, which was then on the Bukiroba station.

While Miriam taught at the Bukiroba Domestic Science School, Phebe went out on safari, giving literacy seminars and setting up her portable bookstore filled with Christian literature at every stop along the way. "We had some good times in that house in Bukiroba," recalls Miriam. "Phebe had retired 'Baraka' because it was so top-heavy, and we used it as a guesthouse. She drove a Volkswagen van. I always thought it was partly her doing that the mission board invited me to go back. That way she was more free to go out on safari."[33]

As Phebe entered her late sixties, her health declined. Although she was still quite strong physically, the first stages of dementia began to affect her communication and interaction with other workers. The Tanzania Mennonite Church, now in the hands of younger men, terminated Phebe's service in early 1969. Miriam Wenger remembers, "Phebe loved to sing. She had this habit that when something didn't go her way, she would leave the room and start singing. When I heard her singing after the meeting that day, I knew it had not gone well."

Under pressure, Phebe agreed to leave Bukiroba and return to McPherson County, Kansas. Finding herself unable to retire quietly, she immediately began to raise her own funds. In November 1969, she bought a one-way plane ticket home to Tanzania, returning as a private citizen. She moved back into her house at Bukiroba.

When Mai (Mama) Yoder, as the Tanzanian villagers respectfully called her, departed her beloved African home for the last time in 1971, several mission workers had to help her board the plane. The tears flow as Miriam tells the story. "Phebe wanted to retire and die in Africa."

Instead, Phebe Yoder surrendered to the ravages of time and the desires of younger mission leaders. She decided to live in New York, joining a Mennonite mission in the city. "She was out on the streets promoting literacy," recalls Mahlon Hess. "The New York folks had lots of praise for her ministry those first years after she came back from Africa."[34]

As the dementia began to erode her senses, Phebe's family finally persuaded her to come home to Kansas. Miriam continues the story: "When we visited her at Schowalter Villa [Hesston, Kansas, retirement community] in 1978, she met me at her door and said, 'I don't know who you are.'

"Before we left, Clyde [Miriam's second husband] suggested we pray in Swahili. It all came flowing back. She was just as sharp as she could be, and there was no confusion."

Phebe Yoder died on September 9, 1981. At her request and in keeping with her lifelong desire to serve others, Phebe's body was donated for medical research to the University Medical Center in Kansas City.[35]

Minnie O. Good

4

I Wrote Irvin's Sermons

Minnie Eberly Holsopple Good
Akron, Pennsylvania

THREE FRESHWATER CREEKS COME together in a shallow gorge near Akron, Pennsylvania. The westward-flowing Cocalico consumes the more narrow Middle Creek, then it widens immediately and cascades straight south another quarter mile before joining Hammer Creek. The three-way intersection forms a redefined Cocalico Creek now running east. In the bend of these east and west waters stands a deserted red-brick house as well as what remains of a small Mennonite truck farm. This is the house where Minnie Eberly, born on November 30, 1908, was raised.

In good times, the fertile bottomland supplied the Eberlys with abundant produce while also supporting livestock such as chickens and hogs. In bad times, it yielded to the common plagues of a flood plain, making the road so muddy no cars could pass, drowning both animals and vegetables, and eventually damaging beyond repair the bridge that connected the Eberly homestead to Millway, a crossroads mill town at the crest of a nearby hill.

"We always had to be alert to high water," recalls Minnie. "Sometimes we got warning of a flood coming from Lebanon County."[1] Because Minnie was the oldest of nine girls with one lone older brother, she inherited many farm-related responsibilities. "I took charge of the chickens. The time the dam broke, Mother woke me up in the middle of the night, 'Minnie, get up right away! The chickens are drowning!' We carried as many as we could up to the mill. That time we had nine inches of water on the kitchen floor. All of us children had to go to different neighbors for the night."

With a bow to their mother who trusted God to look after her children, the Eberlys lived safely in the crook of the creeks for twenty-seven years. As for Minnie, she emerged from her childhood and youth with a certain carefree and confident personality, having learned about hard work and responsibility in the bosom of an unpredictable force of nature.

Minnie's parents, Benjamin and Annie Eberly, were simple country people. Every Sunday they rode their buggy across the Akron hill to Metzler Mennonite Church. "We didn't get a car until I was eight years old," she explains. "Many a time we had to leave the car in Akron and walk home because the road was too muddy back to the farm. Our aunt used to say, 'Oh, the Eberlys are hiking back from Akron again.'"

The rural Mennonites who hiked or drove to the Metzler meetinghouse on most Wednesday evenings, Sunday mornings, and Sunday evenings had a well-defined sense of right Christian living. They believed the basic principles of plain Mennonite faith should be instilled in children at a young age. Unlike many pre-1900 Mennonite teenagers, Minnie and her sisters did not wear fancy clothing prior to their baptism. "I joined the church when I was thirteen, and the only thing I had to change was to start wearing a cape and covering," Minnie shares. "My dresses before that were very simple. What was different in our family was that Father made our clothes."

Trained as a tailor, Minnie's father had his hands in many trades. He loved to sew, piecing over four thousand quilts in his lifetime. He was a farmer, a miller, a quilter, a tailor, and a house painter. "On rainy days he often stayed home," recalls Minnie. "He'd gather all of us girls and teach us how to cut patches for pieced quilts. He sewed the pieces together, and by evening we often had a quilt top made. In later years, women from the sewing circles would come to see him. One time he told a group of visitors that he had made over four thousand quilts. One woman said, 'That's a lie.' Pop looked her in the eye and said, 'I don't lie.'" Such reverence for the principles of domesticity and honesty permeated Minnie Eberly's upbringing.

In the Eberly family, simple living and Bible learning took precedence over higher education. Few went to college, but everyone went to Bible school. Minnie completed a two-year high school Bible course at Eastern Mennonite School in Harrisonburg, Virginia, and came back home to work.

"In those days, the swing of things was the girl-crowds. Twenty to thirty girls would get together at a friend's house on Sunday afternoons," Minnie says. "When they came to our house, we often went swimming down by the dam. In the evening, the boys would come by in their cars and pick up their girlfriends to go to young people's meetings. I always enjoyed watching that. And I always wanted to get married."

As a teenager, Minnie nursed her own mother during the birth of the two youngest children, Mabel and Kathryn. She liked nursing enough to take a job at the Mennonite Home in Lancaster, where she gained practical experience while finishing a mail-order nursing course. As required, she traveled to Chicago for the final two weeks of the course, receiving a license to practice nursing.[2] "It wasn't my first time in a big city," Minnie clarifies. "After we got our car, Pop used to drive us to the Philadelphia Home Mission, where we taught Bible school or Sunday school."

Known for her lighthearted approach to life, Minnie could always tell a good story. One day she laboriously carried several teakettles of hot water to the mission's upstairs bathtub, a necessity in the days before easy access to hot running water. She stepped out of the bathroom briefly. Upon her return, and to her chagrin, Minnie discovered the stopper had not been properly inserted. For the rest of her life, Edna Wenger, Minnie's roommate during one stay at the mission, remembered how Minnie ended the story: "There went the last of my hot water, gooble, gooble, down the drain."[3] Although she liked to enhance a tale with descriptive gestures and silly words, Minnie could also be serious.

After becoming an LPN, she took up home baby nursing, teaching infant care while staying in the homes of new mothers as they adjusted to the overwhelming needs of their newborn children. She enjoyed her work with infants and also worked at the Osteopathic Hospital [now Lancaster's Community Hospital] for awhile. Minnie had a fulfilling career, but she also craved the companionship of a husband and family.

Marriage, however, did not become part of the fabric of her young life. Instead, she led children's classes at rural winter Bible schools in Virginia and West Virginia while continuing her occasional volunteer work for the Philadelphia Home Mission. In her late twenties, Minnie devoted three years to an urban mission in Tennessee. When she arrived at the Mennonite mission in Knoxville, the young children's Sunday school class had four boys. When she left, it had sixteen.[4] After each of these varied Bible teaching experiences, Minnie always came home to the house at Millway, reconnecting smoothly with the placid Mennonite farm life of her family.

The winter before her fortieth birthday, she agreed to serve as matron at the well-regarded Johnstown Bible School (JBS) in west central Pennsylania. Located a few miles south of the city with its infamous flood plain, the Bible school was founded by members of Stahl Mennonite Church. It offered six-week winter Bible courses from 1922-1956. Perfect for farm families, who had more free time after their busy summers of planting and harvesting, JBS attracted hundreds of mainstream Mennonite young people throughout the first half of the twentieth century.

When Minnie arrived at JBS, her younger sister Barbara was already living in Johnstown and working at the newly established Mennonite mission there. Barbara remembers Minnie's first visit: "It is so bleak in Johnstown in the wintertime. Minnie and some of her friends came out together. They made such a fuss how they would never want to live in an area so awful. You know what, they all ended up married and living there. In the summertime, it's very beautiful around Johnstown."[5]

Minnie was in her second winter as matron of JBS when she first noticed Irvin Holsopple. Like many others in the largely rural community, he took an active interest in the ministries of the Bible school. Whenever possible, Irvin enrolled for classes. "I saw this man helping his wife into the church," Minnie explains. "She was sick and had to be on crutches. You know how you sometimes think things to yourself? I thought to myself, 'I hope I find a man as attentive to his wife as he is if I ever get married.'"

Later that year, Barbara wrote the sad news to Minnie that Elizabeth Holsopple had died on September 24, 1949. The patterns of Minnie's day-to-day life would soon change dramatically. In February 1950, she returned to the JBS girls' dorm for her third consecutive winter as matron.

Sometime during that term, Irvin, who was also associate pastor at nearby Kaufman Mennonite Church, became aware of Minnie. Before she left, Irvin and Minnie had discreetly agreed to write to each other. His four children were grown and gone from home. His church community required lots of attention. His farm was labor-intensive. He needed a wife.

Although she was fifteen years younger than Irvin, Minnie was interested. She had admired him from the moment they met, and the wooing did not take long. "I never knew a man as perfect as he was," Minnie says.

Within several months, they discussed marriage and modified their arrangements to fit with the plans of Minnie's sister Ruth. "We stepped up the date of our wedding to May 20 so Ruth could keep her June 10 date. In the 1950s, it was still unusual to have church weddings. We were only the second couple to be married at Metzlers," Minnie recalls. "The reception was at the Akron Fire Hall. I don't remember what we had to eat, but I wore a white wedding dress with black shoes and stockings." In spite of her earlier aversion to its climate and landscape, Minnie moved to Irvin's farm nine miles south of Johnstown.

"I liked being a preacher's wife. Irvin didn't know how to make an outline for his sermons, so I offered to do it for him. You know, I'd be working and I'd have two or three ideas going at a time. I'd stop and write the outline. I was more educated than he was."

Minnie Holsopple's sermon-making was no ordinary case of a preacher's wife giving her husband ideas and supporting him while he studied and prepared his texts. She gathered the ideas, studied the Scripture, wrote the synopses, and finally even preached the sermons in the privacy of their home. On Friday evenings, Irvin would come in from the fields and ask, "Minnie, did you make a sermon ready?"

"Yes, I have one ready, but let's have supper first," she'd say. After supper they would sit side-by-side, perhaps in the living room or on the front porch of their farmhouse.

"The thing is, I preached the sermon to him," Minnie explains. "He would often laugh with me as I went through it because I really expressed myself. I kept telling him, 'Irvin, you have to put more emphasis here. You have to make it live.'

"One evening I remember I was preaching to him, and he just looked at me and started laughing, 'Minnie, you should have been the preacher!'"

She should have been the preacher: it was a sentiment Minnie shared, but in the prevailing current of her 1950s Mennonite world, she could not entertain the thought, not even in her own heart. "I always believed that when you married, you were to be a helpmeet to your husband. I wrote Irvin's sermons. That's how I was his helpmeet." Minnie is offhand, almost dismissive, but her manner does not completely obscure the inherent incongruities in her explanation.

Irvin and Minnie Holsopple would have made a fine husband and wife pastoral team. He was highly regarded for his gentle, insightful spirit and pastoral care gifts, but his public presentations were considered boring. She could make a sermon live, but she had only a limited commitment to the more common caregiving and social tasks usually assigned to a preacher's wife.

"I never liked going to sewing circle," she says bluntly. "I always told Irvin I could stay home and sew quilts much faster than they did at the circle." She stayed home, making hundreds of her own quilts for relief and quietly planning Irvin's Sunday morning sermons. Minnie told a few of her closest friends what she was doing, but most people in the 1950s Johnstown Mennonite community never knew.

A concise description of Irvin Holsopple's life in Sanford Shetler's 1963 history of the Johnstown area distinguished itself in two ways. It elevated Irvin's character far above his proficiency as a preacher, and it made no reference to Minnie's down-home sermon-making. "He was not as strong a man in the pulpit as some, but he had an unimpeachable life which meant much to the church and community. He was a zealous worker, always interested in the church's program, a good attendant at various meetings, and a strong supporter of the doctrines of the Mennonite Church."[6]

Sanford Shetler may not have known about Minnie's sermon-writing gifts, but those who attended Kaufman Mennonite Church in the 1950s noted subtle changes in Irvin's public persona. He became a more interesting preacher after May 1950, they said. Women of the rural congregation occasionally complimented Minnie on Irvin's work, often not knowing that the sermon Irvin had just preached came straight from her.

She loved being married to Irvin. He fit into her family and encouraged her quilt-making energies. Together, they made numerous car trips east along the Pennsylvania Turnpike to her home and the Mennonite Central Committee collection center near Akron. "One time we stopped along the Turnpike at one of those rest places," Minnie says. "When I came back to the car, there was this man staring at the stack of quilts in the backseat. He asked me what they were and what in the world we were doing. I told him they were quilts for relief."

Minnie Holsopple and her sisters carried on the family tradition of making quilts for relief because it was more rewarding than giving money. They did not, however, follow their father's example of keeping a careful record of every quilt pieced and put together. With a touch of ambivalence in her chuckle, Minnie explains, "I made many, many quilts, but I never kept track. So I won't try to say, or I might get in trouble like Pop did."

Then on January 22, 1961, Irvin suffered a heart attack and died. Still an active farmer and pastor, he was only sixty-seven years old. Six months later, Minnie moved back to Lancaster County, bearing the torch of eleven pleasant and productive years, holding the memories of writing her husband's sermons, and hoping to stay connected to her stepchildren and grandchildren. "Irvin's children and grandchildren have always been very kind to me. They still come to see me whenever they can," she says now.

Losing her husband was both disconcerting and shocking for Minnie. Her return to the Lancaster area was marked by a willingness to more fully embrace the community's conscious conservatism. Never a timid personality, she stood up for her beliefs. She knew her Bible and freely expressed her convictions during congregational meetings at Lititz Mennonite Church, where she became a member. She moved to a house on Front Street in Lititz and took a housekeeping position at nearby Linden Hall, a Moravian girls' academy. She continued to sew quilts for relief, piecing as many as one hundred a year.[7]

In 1967, five months before her fifty-ninth birthday, Minnie married Howard Z. Good, a staunchly conservative Lancaster bishop whose first wife died during the birth of their fifth child and whose second wife gave birth to sixteen children before dying in 1957. Howard, who was seventeen years older than Minnie, had been a widower for ten years. "The year before we married, he built that new house along 897 in Cherry Hill. I was the first woman to live in that house."

The preaching partnership Minnie had with Irvin Holsopple never developed with Howard Good. He was a different man and preacher as well as a conservative bishop with an image to uphold. "I asked him whether I could help with his sermons. He told me in no uncertain terms, 'I don't need your help.'"

As it turned out, Howard Good's emphatic rejection of Minnie's offer permanently shut the door on an exercise she had loved. She had married another preacher, but there would be no more writing of sermons for Minnie Good. Eight years later, Howard died after being hit by a car while walking along the busy road not far from their home.

The legends surrounding the composition of Irvin and Minnie Holsopple's sermons will undoubtedly eclipse everything else about Minnie's otherwise ordinary Mennonite story. She could have been a preacher; indeed, she was a preacher. Her husband Irvin stretched the mores of his church and time, letting his wife practice what their community considered an unacceptable gift within the safe parameters of their loving relationship. However, no one but Irvin ever heard Minnie preach.

Following the death of her second husband, Minnie returned to Lititz Mennonite Church where she reconnected to congregational life. Although she never gave sermons at Lititz, she became a stable and known presence in the church, once again sharing her thoughts and opinions in Sunday school classes and congregational meetings.

As she passes age ninety, Minnie Good lives peacefully with her sister Barbara in an apartment along the western edge of the Akron hill, a few miles from the abandoned farm at Millway. She still quilts. She still goes to church as often as possible. And she still remembers and talks about "making Irvin's sermons."

Esther

The Back-Around Work

Esther Mellinger Bair
Hinkletown, Pennsylvania

A BRONZE PLAQUE ABOVE THE inside entrance of the late-twentieth-century Hinkletown Mennonite meetinghouse reads, "In memory of Esther Mellinger Bair conductor of the first summer Bible Schools in this area 1936 and one of the founders of the Hinkletown Mennonite Church 1943."[1] If she were alive, says her friend Grace Wenger, Esther might deflect the honor with a self-effacing laugh and say, "Don't make such a fuss about it. People already think I think too much of myself."[2]

There is no lack of irony in the tribute. History shows she was the visionary behind the church, doing much of the all-consuming mental and physical labor that brought the Hinkletown congregation into being. History also shows she was a lifelong Lancaster Mennonite Conference woman who never held a recognized leadership position in any church, including the one that memorializes her as one of its founders.

Esther Mellinger was born April 6, 1909. Her parents, Aldus and Lydia Mellinger, lived in the Conestoga River village of Hinkletown, Pennsylvania. A relatively well-to-do family with four children, the Mellingers were steeped in Lancaster-area Mennonite ways. Like many of their early 1900s counterparts, they harbored some misgivings about the changes brought on by the Great Awakening, adjusting slowly to the highly defined dress codes and strong new emphasis on spiritual renewal.

An accommodating and easygoing person, Lydia accepted the revival ideas more readily than Aldus. "My grandma had a great desire for the gospel," says Doris Mellinger Sensenig, Esther's niece. "When I was a little girl, we used to go to their house for Sunday dinner. Grandma always wanted everything put away so she could listen to a certain Sunday afternoon radio preacher. But not my grandpa. He wasn't interested in those things."[3]

Fascinated by the intricacies of business and commerce, Aldus taught his children to appreciate the rapid technological advances of the early twentieth century. He brought home a radio when few Mennonite families were buying the talking boxes. He turned his personal curiosity with the Industrial Revolution into a way of putting food on the table and clothes in the closet. With his son, Abe, Aldus founded Conestoga Valley Electric Company, providing electricity to businesses and homes throughout northeastern Lancaster County. An older son, Ben, expanded his father's passion for cars into B. Z. Mellinger Ford, a widely known midcentury auto dealership in New Holland, Pennsylvania.[4]

Daughter Esther, too, acquired an affinity for the new century's innovations. In the 1930s, when few Lancaster Mennonite women ventured behind the wheels of the prized Chevys and Fords owned by the men in their lives, Esther had a car of her own. She drove "with skill and confidence," wrote a friend later.[5]

An apt description of Esther's character as well as her cardriving technique, the phrase "with skill and confidence" encapsulates much of her story. She loved being Mennonite, accepting Jesus at age twelve and receiving baptism and membership at the Ephrata Mennonite meetinghouse on January 15,

1922.[6] She dressed in plain clothing and had a busy social life, participating in an Ephrata-area girl crowd. She had a career, working at the Miller-Hess shoe factory in Akron to save money for a two-year Bible course at Eastern Mennonite School (EMS).[7]

During her youth, Esther also struggled with a recurring health problem. She spent her twenty-third birthday undergoing tests in Philadelphia. The language in a card to her parents reveals a certain lack of self-consciousness in her "countrified" style. "I am sure glad you remembered me on my birthday. Thanks for my nightgown. I guess you got Abram's letter. My stamps are all. I am not feeling so good yesterday and last night. I bleed like everything. But maybe by the time you get this letter I am better. I suppose they are going to give me a transfusion soon. I don't know. Don't worry, I have no pain."[8] A short time later her spleen was removed at a Reading hospital, and Esther gratefully returned to an active and full life.

A simple Mennonite woman, Esther never pursued an education purely for the sake of knowledge, choosing rather to focus on Bible learning. She did not verbalize a theology of leadership, but she knew how to do the work of the church. She liked to joke about being born "on the day Robert Peary discovered the North Pole."[9]

Indeed, there was a streak of the risk-taking explorer in Esther's spirit. Some people thought she was too headstrong, too impulsive, too quick to strike out on her own. The person, perhaps, who worried most about Esther's quick-spiritedness was her more cautious mother.

One adventure made Lydia particularly apprehensive. Esther came home from her first year of Bible training at EMS with a fire in her spirit. Determined to awaken their sleepy farm village, she planned to offer Bible classes to the local children. "This summer I'm going to get some of the Hinkletown children together and teach them Bible stories at our place," was the confident way she described the upcoming project to her EMS roommate, Edna K. Wenger.[10]

Inspired by John L. Stauffer's child Bible study course and undaunted by her mother's concerns, the twenty-five-year-old Esther forged ahead, planning a series of Bible story classes.[11] She went up and down the old Paxton Road (now Route 322), inviting the village children to come and listen.

Lydia watched and wondered. What would the staid Mennonite leaders at their home congregation of Metzler Mennonite Church say? Would they try to stop her daughter? Shouldn't Esther ask the bishop for permission first? "I remember hearing Grammy Mellinger and my mother talking on the phone," recounts Esther's niece Ruth Horst Herr. "They were wondering what would happen if Esther would do such a thing."[12]

It was not in Esther Mellinger's nature to wait for permission when she saw work that needed to be done. She bought Bible school supplies with her own money, cleaned up her brother's electrical shop, and persuaded her nieces and nephews to come so the town children would not feel alone or strange. During that Great Depression summer of 1934, the word quickly spread. The children came. Esther took a group photo and labeled it "Children's Meeting, Summer 1934," assuring that the narrative of the first Hinkletown Bible School would not be forgotten.[13] By the second summer, the school had far outgrown the shop at the Mellinger home. Where, Esther wondered, could they meet in 1935?

She soon had a plan. About a mile east of the Hinkletown Mill stood an ancient decaying structure—the Bethel union church. Conceived by a circuit-riding Church of God preacher and chiefly bankrolled by a local doctor, the building had first served the community in 1837, nearly one hundred years earlier.[14] Like other union churches, it was open to any Protestant denomination, filling an important function in a village never affluent or populous enough to support the large number of church buildings—Lutheran, Mennonite, Methodist, and Presbyterian—found in many other Lancaster County towns.

Following a deed dispute between the doctor and the preacher in the mid-1850s, the building gradually lost its shine. By the time Esther thought of meeting in the church, Mennonites and other locals used it sporadically, as the grounds gave way to dandelions and crabgrass and the structure faded from lack of care.

Setting her sights on revitalizing the little country church, Esther rallied a group of family members and friends for a community cleanup project. Rolling up her sleeves, she pulled weeds, scrubbed floors and walls, and once again spread the word. The Hinkletown Bible School had a new home.

Every Thursday night for the next three summers (1935-1938) the old union church sanctuary came alive with flannelgraph Bible stories and spirited Bible school choruses. In 1935 Esther Mellinger and her friend, Esther Sensenig, were the only teachers for the sixty-plus eager youngsters who came looking for love. The renewal of the neighborhood church brought a parallel awakening to the hearts of many Hinkletown children—children whose surnames suggest they came from an assortment of ethnic and religious backgrounds.[15] As the attendance multiplied, Esther Mellinger realized she needed more help.

Beginning in 1936, she asked her younger brother, Abe, and their friend, John S. Wenger, to serve as superintendents. Although the three young people cooperated in managing the school, Esther did most of the legwork, shopping for supplies, cleaning the church, and inviting the children. She usually led the singing, blending her melodic voice into the group as the unforgettable songs of summer Bible school rang out from the red-brick church: "Come to Bible school, come to Bible school," and "Our Bible School is over, and we are going home. Good-bye, good-bye, be always kind and good."

True to form, traditional local Mennonites began to ask questions. Some furrowed their brows because of the youthful leaders and the absence of ordained men. After a deputation from Groffdale visited the Bible school in 1938, Abe, Esther, and John reluctantly agreed to move the Bible school from Hinkletown to Groffdale Mennonite Church.[16] Although the three mourned the loss of their convenient village location, they packed their cars with Hinkletown children, and for many summers bounced across the winding roads to Groffdale.

In a demonstration of grace that would come to distinguish each of their adult lives, they gave their full support to the ordained leaders who took over the work. John Wenger agreed to be co-superintendent. Abe Mellinger taught a class. Esther told a friend, "I'll just do the back-around work."[17] She also taught a nursery class and each evening led the traditional closing song.

Back in Hinkletown, the community people missed the regular summer services in their union church. Maybe they could have Sunday school in the local church. Were the Mennonites interested?

Once again, Esther, Abe, and John put their heads together. Years later John called Esther the "person of vision." God had laid it on her heart to reopen the church, he said. It was she who never stopped hoping Hinkletown would have its own Mennonite congregation. It was she who articulated the basic concern—the people of this small town, many of whom were not involved in church life, needed a convenient and visible place to come and worship. The three former leaders of the Hinkletown Bible School decided to approach the recently ordained Groffdale bishop, Mahlon Witmer.

Revered for his gentle, loving spirit, Mahlon was appreciated by many Lancaster Mennonite women. In the case of Esther Mellinger and the Bethel union church, he cast his full support behind her burden—a burden she articulated and held with clear vision. The people of Hinkletown, she said, needed a place to worship. The little red-brick church with its altar rail, classic pews, and matching cannon coal stoves seemed the perfect solution.[18]

On Sunday, August 1, 1943, Esther, Abe, John, and their families and friends assembled for an all-day inauguration on the grounds of the spruced-up union church. Bishop Witmer preached the morning sermon entitled "The People Had a Mind to Work." An Amish Mennonite brother who drove up from Morgantown to share in the service remarked, "When I used to pass this empty church and see its condition, it looked to me as if the wrath of God dwelt on that place. Now the grace of God has moved in."[19]

The grace of God personified by Esther Mellinger, Abe Mellinger, and John S. Wenger had indeed moved into the little church. All three became intimately involved in lay leadership. Esther taught a Sunday school class and dedicated herself to the "back-around work."

Once a week, Esther, her nephew Lester Horst, and Mary Good, one of the young people, cleaned the church. Mary Good remembers, "There were two pot-bellied stoves, one on the women's side and one on the men's side. Esther would drive up to S. H. Good's planing mill for a bag of little pieces of wood, and sometimes we had a bag of coal in the car. Sometimes we started the fire on Friday evening and sometimes not until Saturday. Once a month we went down to Weaver's bookstore near Blue Ball to get Sunday school ticket rewards."[20]

When Bishop Witmer asked John S. Wenger to be Sunday school superintendent, John agreed on the condition that he and Abe be appointed co-superintendents with equal standing. He had too often seen others gather power to themselves, John said, when they were given sole leadership positions. John's request was rooted in the unusual threefold partnership that he, Abe, and Esther had created, but it also foretold a congregational trait of mutual leadership and shared strength that would become the whole cloth of God's grace at the little country church.

In addition to her work at the church, Esther continued her factory career at Miller-Hess. As she moved through her thirties, visits with family and friends filled her days. People knew her as someone who willingly dropped in to share with those who were suffering. In a *Gospel Herald* article she wrote, "Certainly visits are appreciated by all who can and may have company. I am sure if that is not available a card has meant more to you who are shut in than you can tell."[21] She made regular car trips to the public library in Lancaster, coming home with "stacks of books because she and my grandma loved to read," remembers niece Ruth Horst Herr.[22]

When Lydia Mellinger became ill in 1945, Esther quit her job to stay home and care for her. All four children—Anna, Ben, Esther, and Abe—with their father and spouses sat by their mother's bedside when she slipped from the world at 10:35 p.m. on March 26, 1945.[23]

Two weeks later, the trustees of the old union church, including a great-granddaughter of the doctor who had financed the building, transferred the deed without restrictions to the Mennonites. Two years later, the congregation requested an ordination to solidify its status as a full-fledged church.

John and Abe were both in the lot. So was an accomplished young speaker and Bible teacher named Warren Good. The bishop oversight committee hesitated because of Warren's less rigid views on church discipline. Mahlon Witmer asked John

Wenger, "Shall we take Warren through?" John answered, "If Warren doesn't go through, I don't go through either." On June 4, 1947, the lot fell on Warren Good.[24] Once again, the grace of God blessed the Hinkletown church. Warren's dynamic preaching brought the congregation to full bloom. With her beloved church in capable hands, Esther Mellinger moved on to another chapter in her story.

Later that summer of 1947, she left a Mellinger family reunion uncharacteristically early. The next day Ruth Horst asked her mother why Aunt Esther disappeared so quickly. Aunt Esther, it turned out, had a date with Landis Bair. He was a fifty-four-year-old grandfather and widower from Carpenter Mennonite Church with three daughters—Anna Ruth, Miriam, and Martha. Although he was sixteen years her senior, Esther and Landis were married before the end of August 1947.

"They just went over to Mahlon Witmer's house, and he married them at home," her niece Ruth remembers. "Then the Mellingers had a big shower at Uncle Ben's. I remember someone gave them a pair of bears. Esther held them up and made a fuss about the 'the bear family.'"[25] Esther transferred her belongings a few miles west and south to Landis Bair's Brownstown home and her church membership about an equal distance to Carpenter Mennonite Church.

It was a whole new world for Esther Bair. Miriam and Martha were still at home. No longer a woman with a career, Esther had to adjust to keeping house with her stepdaughters. She also participated more regularly in the traditional women's side of church life. The Carpenter sewing circle alternated among members' homes and met on the last Saturday afternoon of each month.

One Saturday Esther was late to sewing circle. Frustrated with herself, she sat down and rapidly began sewing to make up for lost time. Only when the old treadle machine's bobbin fell out did she stop. Laughing exuberantly, she admitted to "working so hard the machine flew apart."[26]

Esther Mellinger Bair knew how to laugh at herself. Her direct and openly physical temperament sometimes caught people off guard. Another day when the sewing circle met, Esther again arrived a bit late. The other women sat in a large circle, politely avoiding the family's comfortable platform rocker. Esther strode into the room, thanked everyone for leaving the best seat for her, and threw herself into the chair. Both the chair and Esther promptly fell over backward. There she lay flat on her back and kicking her feet in the air as she tried to force the chair to become upright again. The entire roomful of women succumbed to helpless laughter. Several came to her aid, but Esther just kept flailing her legs and laughing. Finally, someone managed to turn the chair on its side and Esther crawled out. For years the Carpenter sewing circle joked about saving the "best chair for Esther Bair."[27]

On her first Christmas Eve as a Bair family member, stepdaughter Miriam married Leon Buckwalter. A year later Esther and Landis were seeking to adopt a child of their own. In February 1949 they brought home son Mark to join his stepsister Martha, now in her late teens. Esther turned forty two months later and settled into the routines of a busy mother and wife.

At Carpenter she taught the nursery class in Sunday school, influencing the work of the church, as she always had, in her direct but unthreatening way. When Richard and Gail Kling lost their six-year-old daughter in 1953, Esther rallied the congregation to raise $148 for round-trip air fare so the Klings' home minister, Michael N. Wenger, could attend the funeral. The Klings had been commissioned by Carpenter to serve a church planting in Freemanville, Alabama.[28]

It was also Esther's idea to establish a "cradle roll department" at Carpenter. Every year at the church business meeting, two women were appointed to enroll newborns in the cradle roll and present their parents with a gift from the congregation. Until the tiny toddlers entered the nursery class, they received annual birthday cards from the cradle roll department. As long as Esther chaired this branch of the Carpenter Sunday school, she always used her own money to purchase the cards and gifts.[29]

Sometime in the 1950s, Esther and Landis decided to convert part of their spacious Brownstown home into a convalescent center. Reviving her longtime concern for shut-ins, Esther took on the challenge of nursing as many as twelve to fourteen aging residents at a time. They hired a small staff, but the ever-energetic Esther did much of the work. Landis's daughter Martha married Ben Hershey on April 22, 1956. Young Mark Bair grew up in the nursing home.

After abruptly becoming very ill in December 1966, Esther Mellinger Bair died of cancer on Valentine's Day in 1967. She was only fifty-seven. With the help of the staff, Landis kept the nursing center open several more years until all those for whom Esther had cared passed on or found new homes. "This," wrote her dear friend Edna K. Wenger later, "was as Esther would have wanted it."[30]

Seventeen years after her premature death, one of Esther's nieces described her much-admired aunt: "She was a person with great compassion, energy, and vision, often frustrated by the events of life but seldom daunted. A strong lady, one I miss very much."[31]

Catharine Leatherman

6

Will You
Go with Me to Africa?

Catharine Garber Leatherman
Bukiroba, Tanzania and Mount Joy, Pennsylvania

BOTH OF CATHERINE GARBER'S parents were schoolteachers. When they married, Ada Garber took up homemaking and Henry farming, but they never stopped encouraging their three children—Catharine, born June 30, 1914, Robert, and Lois—to pursue knowledge and learning. The Garbers also taught their children to cherish the church, and like many Lancaster Mennonites during the first half of the twentieth century, the Garber family was completely immersed in Bible study and worship.

As a young child, Catharine once proudly turned to her father while they were milking the family cows and declared, "I know everything in the Bible."[1]

His eyes twinkled. "You do? Then who is Melchizedek?" Not knowing the answer was one of Catharine Garber's first lessons in humility, but she also resolved to learn and remember the correct response.

Reading the Bible—and every other book in her parent's library—held together much of Catharine's early life experience. She eagerly attended the local public school. When she felt the call of Jesus at age nine, Henry and Ada persuaded her to wait a few years before making a public confession. She was a missionary-in-the-making, a young girl whose interests and pursuits foreshadowed a focused dedication to faithful living.

During her childhood and youth, Catharine's father spent many hours away from home, attending to his church-related responsibilities. He had been ordained to the pastoral ministry at their family church, Mount Joy Mennonite. He also served the Eastern Mennonite Board of Missions and Charities, which had officially organized the year Catharine was born. He found fulfillment in church work, actively speaking out for the establishment of a foreign mission work, perhaps in Africa. Once when the Eastern Board treasurer, Sem Eby, pointed out that the Africa fund contained a scant $9.62, Henry Garber stood up, flashed his soft smile, and said, "But we have a large stock of faith."[2]

Whenever the church beckoned, Henry relied on his oldest daughter to milk the cows and help the younger children with farm chores; in typical teenage fashion, she resented the extra work. She also lamented the time her father spent away from the family. "I was very blessed, though, to have a father who constantly challenged me to learn and grow, to live up to my full potential," Catharine says now.

When she graduated from high school, Catharine pled with her parents to let her attend Mansfield College in northeastern Pennsylvania where she could study domestic science (also called home economics). Her parents, however, firmly guided her toward Eastern Mennonite School. "I wasn't elated about this because EMS offered only a two-year liberal arts program at that time," says Catharine. "I didn't think it was what I wanted."

Nevertheless, Catharine obediently headed for EMS in Virginia's Shenandoah Valley, where she supplemented a two-year Bible course with teacher training classes. By the time she exhausted the educational possibilities at EMS, Catharine

needed one more year to complete a B.S. in elementary education. "Although I remembered the domestic science dreams, I
knew the path my parents recommended had definitely
changed my life for the better."

One of those changes was precipitated by her growing attraction to John Leatherman, a fellow student from Doylestown, Pennsylvania. Unlike Henry Garber, John's father had
given him little support for pursuing Bible education. Asher
Leatherman wanted John to follow in his footsteps and work at
a desk in Philadelphia's busy downtown train station, the Reading Terminal. Against his father's wishes, John sold his car and
moved to Virginia to study the Bible.

Just before Christmas in his second year at EMS, John
found himself facing ordination by lot at his home church in
Doylestown. When the lot fell to John, the bishop asked him to
give up the last semester of his education and return home to
work for the church. Encouraged by some members of the congregation, John decided to try doing both. He promised to
make the five-hundred-mile round-trip once a month to deliver
a Sunday morning sermon. "Don't ask me how he managed all
of that," says Catharine. "I do remember one time, he got a ride
in the back of someone's truck. It was winter. Later, he told me
he had never been so cold in all his life. I felt for him so much,
because I was enjoying our friendship more and more."

Ever true to her own sense of call, Catharine left EMS in
1934. She went home to Mount Joy to complete her degree
work at the nearby Elizabethtown College. Although she never
breathed a word of her convictions to anyone, Catharine felt
certain in her heart of two things: God was calling her to Africa,
and she was in love with John Leatherman. "What I didn't know
was how those two things would ever come together."

Earlier that year, Henry Garber had agreed to become
chair of the Eastern Board. The much-talked-about plans to

send Lancaster Mennonite missionaries to Africa rapidly became reality. By the summer of 1934, the first workers—Elam and Elizabeth Stauffer and John and Ruth Mosemann—had already set up a mission station at Shirati in the Lake Victoria region of Tanganyika. The Eastern Board gave the work high priority, asking various young people in the Lancaster and Souderton-area communities to consider the call. Bishop Noah Mack approached John Leatherman about becoming a possible candidate, but John had a more immediate concern. He needed to talk to Catharine Garber.

"'Will you go with me to Africa?' That's how John asked me to marry him. 'Will you go with me to Africa?'" Catharine recalls. The two goals most dear to Catharine Garber—an open door to Africa and freedom to marry John Leatherman—merged in that memorable moment. To her, John's question was a sign of God's presence and care for the details of life.

Catharine finished the school year at Elizabethtown, graduating in the class of 1935 with a degree in elementary education. She celebrated her twenty-first birthday on June 30 and married John, who was five years older, in a simple ceremony at the Garber home on September 7.

Seven months later John and Catharine Leatherman set sail for Africa—two fresh-faced young missionaries with clear directions from Eastern Board to "start a teacher training school" and high hopes for learning Swahili quickly. John had been ordained. Catharine had a teaching degree. He carried the church credentials, she the education credentials. Though it was never openly articulated or officially written, the Leathermans expected they would work as a team.

"At the time we left for Africa, we had a farewell meeting in my home church [Mount Joy]," Catharine says. "Various men made speeches. Henry Lutz—he was the bishop at that time—got up and said, 'I think it would be all right if Sister Catharine would stand up where she is and say a few words.' Now that was unheard of—a woman speaking in church. But Sister Catharine stood up and said a few words."

Henry Lutz's recognition of Catharine's calling, though perhaps unintended, became the first stitch in a strong seam that attached her education and leadership gifts to her everyday experiences in East Africa. "John always encouraged and included me," she recalls. "When we had our first church council in Bukiroba, he asked me to go with him to the meeting. 'You are part of this, too,' he said." Along with other mission workers, she and John soon discovered there was more than enough to do—for both women and men. From the beginning, Catharine's ministry and teaching gifts were needed and used.

The Bukiroba station, with its stunning view of Mara Bay from a hill above Lake Victoria, took both Catharine and John by surprise when they arrived on June 22, 1936. They were impressed with the light-filled beauty of their new home. In some ways, the Leathermans adjusted quickly. John packed away his formal, plain-cut suit and black wool hat and took to wearing short-sleeved white shirts and a sun helmet. He made himself comfortable, establishing connections in the nearby port town of Musoma and its surrounding villages.

Other adjustments were more difficult. The way African women wrapped cloth around their bodies seemed a strange way of dressing to the Leathermans. The women's elaborate jewelry troubled John and Catharine's sense of simplicity. One day Catharine spoke up. "I told several women that what they needed to do was take off their ornaments—those earrings and the big heavy brass bracelets on their ankles and arms."

The women were not impressed. "If you take off your ornaments, we'll take off ours."

"Me? I don't have ornaments!" Sixty years later, Catharine Leatherman laughs merrily as she relates this moment in her orientation to the culture and people of Tanganyika. The women meant her corrective eye glasses. It was only one of many occasions in which African women helped Catharine catch a glimpse of the many dimensions of human experience.

The lifestyle of eastern Pennsylvania Mennonites sometimes clashed with the centuries-old rhythm of Tanganyikan village life. For the missionaries, these encounters raised a sea of questions. How do you explain the Holy Kiss in a culture where kissing is unknown? How do you tell poor people with no sewing machines to turn their colorful, draping cloth into plain dresses? How do you tell men who live and work on the edge of the Equator to wear long trousers? How do you explain stockings and closed-toe shoes to people who prefer bare feet? These were only a few of the dilemmas the missionaries faced as they began to interact with Africans and as these new friendships challenged their Lancaster Mennonite doctrines and ideas.

The Bukiroba teacher training school opened on October 14, 1936, albeit in humble circumstances. Three students from Shirati, along with their wives, were housed in the car garage next to John and Catharine's two-room, grass-roofed home. Zedekia Kisare, who later became a respected bishop in the Tanzania Mennonite Church, and his wife Susana, slept in the bed of the mission pickup.[3] Catharine was pregnant with her first child, but she joined in teaching a small group of locals how to read Swahili. She also participated with John in guiding the Shirati students through a curriculum of Bible, geography, and health courses.

Zedekia Kisare later described how he experienced Catharine's teaching gifts: "I found Catharine Leatherman's Old Testament courses particularly interesting, for I found so many parallels between our Luo society at Kiseru and those ancient people of God."[4] Catharine's dream of working as a teacher in Africa had materialized.

On February 16, 1937, she labored through the birth of their first daughter, Lois, in their small hut. Later the mission built a more permanent mud-brick place, where the Leathermans lived for most of their twenty-nine years in Tanzania. In her first decade in Africa, Catharine's world expanded dramatically. She became a mother to four children—Lois, William, Andrew, and Stephen. While the children kept her busy, they did not interrupt the flow of her many other responsibilities as a teacher and nurse. "I wasn't trained as a nurse, but I could dispense aspirin and medicines for the common village ailments," she points out now. "Every morning in the years before our mission had a clinic, I would step outside my home and minister to as many as twenty patients who had come for help. Always I tried to point them to Jesus."

Catharine also gave much of her missionary life to being a hostess. Because Bukiroba was only six miles from the Lake Victoria harbor at Musoma, the station served as a port of entry for arriving missionaries, Eastern Board delegations, and countless other foreigners passing through East Africa. Catharine served delicious meals, provided beds, and extended a homespun brand of hospitality and warmth. "As we sat there in the Leatherman living room recalling times past, one almost thought we were back in Lancaster County," is how Miriam and Ray Wenger remembered their own first evening in Tanganyika, East Africa.[5]

Most welcome of the early visitors were the members of the 1938 Lancaster mission board deputation—Bishop Henry Lutz, Eastern Board chair Henry Garber, and his wife Ada. Catharine and Ada treasured the mother-daughter time. Henry and Ada met their small granddaughter for the first time. Henry Lutz and Henry Garber asked questions and gave advice. As the group traveled among the mission compounds, the Tanganyika mission workers gratefully took advantage of their first opportunity to express their many concerns about cultural differences to these people from home.

Back in Lancaster County, the Mennonite community eagerly awaited the delegation's return, hoping for a report filled with stories of many souls being saved. Such a report was not forthcoming— primarily because few, if any, Tanganyikan villagers thought of themselves as lost souls. Most were members of strong, virile tribes with ancient, though unwritten, histories. They lined up to receive the services of the strange white missionaries often for very practical reasons: they needed work and money, they were sick, they wanted an education, or they were curious.

As John and Catharine Leatherman and the other missionaries integrated their faith into daily life, the core tenets of Christianity began to appeal to some of the local folks around the mission compounds. Although small ripples of change had appeared by that summer of 1938, the forecasted waves desired by Mennonites back home were no longer on the immediate horizon.

Before the deputation left Tanganyika, they conducted an ordination, giving Elam Stauffer a charge of bishop and the fledgling mission a level of autonomy. Bishop Lutz and the Garbers returned to Lancaster with a simple report that all was progressing slowly but well on the Mennonite mission field in East Africa.

By 1941, the Tanganyika mission embraced five stations: Bumangi, Bukiroba, Mugango, Nyabasi, and Shirati. Eight young couples, three single women, and a lively group of expatriate children filled the houses and grounds, forming little Mennonite villages in the grassy hills above Lake Victoria.[6]

Late that year as the United States entered the fray of World War II, transatlantic passenger travel became very difficult. John and Ruth Mosemann were caught stateside, unable to return to the Shirati station. The next people in line for home leave, the Leatherman family and Phebe Yoder, were told by the Eastern Board not to attempt passage across the war-torn Atlantic shipping corridor. Regular mail service took as long as three to five months, and airmail letters were much too expensive. The missionaries began to feel isolated and removed from their families and homes.

Discouragement and depression set in. Twelve of the small group of Tanganyikan believers at Bukiroba fell away from the faith. "We thought we were bringing Jesus to our African brothers and sisters," remembers Catharine. "What had gone wrong? We began to ask ourselves why we had so little spiritual discernment."

Then a renewal movement washed over several other Protestant missions in the Lake Victoria region, and a season of soul-searching brought new energy and life to the Mennonites who had come to East Africa. "I think it started in Rwanda where one Anglican mission worker and one African brother got together," says Catharine. "The Lord began showing them they needed to be open with one another and repent of their wrong attitudes."

The missionaries who lived and worked on the scattered Mennonite stations responded in their own ways to the urgent calls for revival. Some resisted. Some, like John and Catharine Leatherman, slowly yielded to a complete infusion of the Holy Spirit. "It took about five years for me to let go of my belief that I was 'good.' It was a watershed in my life," Catharine says with conviction now. "It's not just some incident that happened a long time ago. The Lord came to me and showed me that the African brothers and sisters and I were on the same level. I no longer saw myself as someone reaching a hand down to people in a ditch. We're all down in the ditch, and we're finding that Jesus is the way out, so we give testimony to that."

The revival also affected John, who changed "from being church-centered to being Christ-centered," recalls Catharine. "He repented of his wrong attitudes toward Africans. They loved it. Pastor Leatherman, they said, became one of them. He was softer. For me, it was letting go of my self-centeredness. God showed me a mountain of selfishness, of trampling on others. I thought I was free of outward acts of sin, but God showed me hypocrisy. Three days after consenting to the death of my proud old person, an overwhelming joy came to me. I still struggle with self, but it does not rule my life. I learned to love; I learned to really love the Tanganyikans who were my students, who became my sisters and brothers in Christ."

In August 1944, with the war still in full force, John and Catharine with their four small children and Phebe Yoder boarded a Lake Victoria steamer in Musoma. Following a complex overland route by lake steamer and train, they made their way to Capetown, South Africa, where passage had been reserved on a neutral ship across the South Atlantic. Everything moved with amazing smoothness until they reached Capetown. "Because it was neutral, our ship had no priority. It needed repairs. We waited four and a half months in Capetown."

After only two of those months had passed, the Leatherman family stared into the empty space of homelessness. Capetown was filled with people, and rooms to rent were hard to come by. "Then this dear lady I had met asked us to her house for tea," Catharine recounts. "She was the founder of the African Evangelistic Band. She invited us to stay in the two anterooms at the back of their chapel. They loaned us cots, dishes, and this little kerosene stove where I did our cooking." Finally, after another ten weeks, they sailed for Buenos Aires.

The Leatherman boys were two, four, and five, and daughter Lois celebrated her eighth birthday on the trip. Catharine and John spent most of the twenty-day crossing worrying about the children's safety. The ship's loading deck, designed to transport cargo and not passengers, was protected only by two chains. It fell straight off into the sea. "You couldn't just let them play like they wanted to because falling off the deck was a real possibility," recalls Catharine.

Five months after leaving their house in Bukiroba, the Leathermans and Phebe Yoder disembarked in Argentina, only to wait another three weeks for flight reservations to the States. They visited various South American Mennonite missions.

The small group of traveling missionaries finally left Buenos Aires on three different flights to Miami. After reconnecting in Miami, they took a train to Philadelphia, where Catharine's parents met them at the 30th Street Station.[7] "That first trip home was quite a trek. It was, it was, it was." Catharine's voice registers the utter relief and weariness of a mother who had managed to safely shepherd four small children across an ocean and three continents in a time of war—from a safe, familiar place above Lake Victoria to another safe, familiar place in the rolling farmland adjoining the Susquehanna River.

John and Catharine settled in to enjoy their yearlong furlough. Henry and Ada listened to their stories. The Eastern Board and the Bishop Board asked them questions. Mennonite churches throughout southeastern Pennsylvania invited John to talk about the work in Tanganyika. Sometimes Catharine was also asked to speak in these churches. One pastor, Melvin Lauver, put them both on the program at his church, Lititz Mennonite, and asked Catharine to go up on the raised platform to speak. "That was something women didn't do in Mennonite churches," Catharine says. "It just wasn't done. I don't think I stood behind the pulpit. I stood beside it. But that was the first time I ever experienced speaking from the pulpit.

"It's interesting to see how doors open," Catharine reflects. "Neither John nor I thought you could push down a door, or force it open, or kick it open. But when it opens, you went through. So it just happens that in ministry, I've been able to go through a few doors as they opened for the first time."

Sometimes neither Catharine nor John knew whether their message of personal renewal was being heard. At a church in Bally, Pennsylvania, Catharine felt called to speak clearly and directly. "I told the people how I found Jesus in Africa, how I had been convicted to let go of my own selfish desires and wishes. 'You must die to self and be joined to Jesus in life.' Afterwards, I couldn't understand why no one responded to me. They were all so silent. I agonized for a long time about whether I had done the right thing. Yet I never heard from anyone in that congregation."

Fifty years later, however, someone did respond. "I was sitting on a bench here at Landis Homes when a woman sat down next to me. 'Catharine, I remember something you said in my church at Bally fifty years ago. You said we must die to self. That message changed my life.'"

Catharine Leatherman's soft preacher eyes fill with tears as she remembers. "This was such a great encouragement to me. Fifty years later! You never know. When the Lord gives you something to say, say it."

The Leathermans returned to Bukiroba in June 1946. For the next nineteen years, John ministered to and taught Bible school students from Shirati to Bumangi and Bukiroba to Mugango. He also gave pastoral leadership to various emerging Mennonite churches. Catharine continued her work as a hostess, mother, and teacher, imparting everything from basic language skills and Bible theology to cooking lessons and sewing tips. "All the years we were in Africa I taught the Bible, mainly to women's groups. I have felt that the most significant part of my work was with these women, many of them the wives of church leaders."[8]

As the years passed, Catharine, John, and the children grew to appreciate the different flavors and sounds of Tanganyika. They enjoyed *ugali*, a stiff mush dipped into vegetables or meat; *mchicha*, a dish of mixed greens; and the distinctive tea with lots of milk and sugar. Swahili slipped from their tongues with ease. "Once, though, when John was preaching he meant to say, 'Oh that I had a voice like thunder!' What he actually said was, 'Oh that I had a voice like a pig,'" Catharine recalls with a laugh. "The congregation was so respectful. Maybe they laughed about it later, but at the time no one even snickered."

Together they cared for and nourished their family of four. As the children turned fourteen or fifteen, Catharine and John thought they should get some of their schooling in the United States. Each time they left one of their children in the States after a furlough, Catharine says it was difficult—both for child and parents.

"Leaving my children was *the* most difficult thing in my whole mission life," says Catharine now. "I have been most grateful that these children from whom we separated all came to love the Lord. It means a great deal to me." Of all the work Catharine and John accomplished on the mission field, their greatest concern always lay with their children, the four young souls they had raised in Tanganyika and guided to their American homeland as adults.

In August 1963, five days after his twenty-first birthday, their youngest son, Steve, crashed his motorcycle on a country road in Lancaster County. He was permanently paralyzed from the neck down. "We were still in Africa. This was one of the great sorrows of our life," Catharine says. A year and a half later, the Eastern Board released John and Catharine from their missionary commitments in Africa, and they returned to the Garber home in Mount Joy. Their son Steve went to a rehabilitation center in Johnstown, where he met his wife. They adopted a daughter, who now lives in Lancaster and is the grandchild closest in proximity to Catharine. Steve died in April 1980.

The years following John and Catharine's 1965 leave-taking of Bukiroba were touched by both joy and sorrow, by pain and pleasure. John considered several pastorates in the Franconia Conference, but neither Catharine nor John felt God's call to Franconia. Their first responsibility, they believed, lay with their son and Catharine's aging parents in Lancaster County.

Then Catharine's mother died, and her father, who was blind, didn't want to go to a retirement community as they had planned. Catharine and John considered whether they should stay in her parents' house and make a home for her father. "He had done so much for us," says Catharine simply. "So we did that."

John took a job as a laborer. "Raymond Charles felt John's ministry should be officially recognized in the Lancaster Conference," she recalls. "So in the last year of his life, John's Franconia ordination was transferred to the Lancaster Conference. John was quite a Bible teacher. That was his calling and his gift." In May 1969, John passed away after being diagnosed with pancreatic cancer.

"Looking back, I have great gratitude that we didn't move to any of those Franconia churches. When John died, I was in my own conference, among my friends and relatives, in my home church." For this Lancaster Mennonite woman, who gave twenty-nine years to mission work in another country and culture, it was an especially poignant way to let go of the one constant presence through that time, her beloved John.

The years since her husband's death have been filled with activity and blessing. "I took a job as the first social worker and volunteer coordinator at Landis Homes. As I had done in Africa, I continued to teach the Bible—to Sunday school classes, women's retreats, and small groups. I think my mission experience gave me a sort of special status and perhaps helped open doors for some other women."

A pastor in Catharine's home congregation at Mount Joy surprised her one day in the early 1990s. "How would you feel about becoming a deaconess?" he asked.

"Just what would the duties be?"

"Oh, you'd keep right on doing what you've been doing," he responded.

She agreed and was licensed as a deaconess in 1991. Catharine's trademark chuckle does not conceal the awe she feels at receiving credentials for ministry, a validation of her gifts from the congregation where she was born and raised.

In 1997 she sold her family home in Mount Joy and moved to the Landis Homes Retirement Community. In the living room of her humbly furnished apartment, she shares the story of her life and "the star upon which I've guided my craft. I've wanted to bring my whole life under the lordship of Jesus Christ." Seventy-five years have passed since Catharine's first encounter with Jesus as a nine-year-old. The language of her salvation has not changed. Neither has its encompassing reality.

Mary H. Lauver

The Lord Put
the Ideas in My Mind

Mary Hottenstein Lauver
Akron, Pennsylvania

THOSE LANCASTER MENNONITES WHO at the middle of the twentieth century were convinced women of their denomination were not involved in church leadership must not have known Mary Hottenstein Lauver. Perhaps they never attended any of her craft-making classes, her inspirational talks, or the Lititz Mennonite Church, where for thirty years she served beside her pastor husband, Melvin Lauver. Although she never preached, she worked as a partner with Melvin, standing by him and sharing in decision making as he gave direction and leadership to this small-town Lancaster Mennonite congregation.

The second child and only daughter of Wallace and Mary Brubaker Hottenstein, Mary was born March 31, 1916. As a child, she learned to exercise the rather different disciplines of creativity and responsibility. Responsibility was taught in the everyday tasks of church and farm life. Her parents owned a family farm near East Petersburg, Pennsylvania, and her father was ordained deacon at East Petersburg Mennonite Church when Mary was seventeen.

The lessons about creativity came from her mother. "If I wanted a new pocketbook, for instance, my mother was likely to get me material for making one. I learned to use my ingenuity and tried to turn out a finished product I would find satisfaction in using."[1] Both Mary Hottensteins—mother and daughter—enjoyed fashioning useful things from throwaways such as ice cream containers, coffee cans, or typewriter ribbon boxes. The ice cream containers became sewing or knitting chests, the coffee cans became little wishing-well planters, and the typewriter ribbon boxes became pin keepsakes.[2]

In the spring of 1934, daughter Mary graduated from East Hempfield High School. Two years later she agreed to a date with Melvin Lauver after he noticed her at the East Petersburg Mennonite meetinghouse during an evening revival service. Melvin explains, "I had been dating another girl, and we talked about getting married. But I just didn't have peace about it, so even though it was hard, I broke off our friendship. Sometime later Mary and I started dating. Looking back, I am just so thankful. I know it was definitely the leading of the Lord that Mary and I got together."[3] Mary Hottenstein and Melvin Lauver were married at East Petersburg on August 18, 1938.

The first years of their marriage, coming on the heels of the Great Depression, required further creativity as well as frugality from both Mary and Melvin. Trained in finances, Melvin landed a job at the local Akron Bank. When it came time to find a house to buy, he researched various options, deciding it was most cost-effective to design and build their own house. He bought a lot at what would become 1033 Broad Street in Akron, hired a carpenter, and went at the task with the enthusiasm and purpose of a young man wanting to please the woman he loved.

Three and a half years after Mary and Melvin's wedding, the United States responded to the bombing of Pearl Harbor by joining the melee that was World War II. Melvin was drafted. Early in 1942 he reported to a Civilian Public Service (CPS) Camp operated by Mennonite Central Committee (MCC) in

Luray, Virginia. Mary stayed home in Akron. "Some of the men teased me about my wife back home, but Mary and I understood our arrangement. That's what mattered," says Melvin.

After Melvin transferred to a recently opened camp in Montana, he requested that his wife be permitted to join him. "I came home for Christmas 1942. We rented our house, and Mary went back to Montana with me. They asked Mary to be dietitian for the camp. She trained cooks, and I was the business manager. I was so glad to have her there with me."

In January 1946, the Lauvers moved from the mountains of Montana to the tropical La Plata River valley in Puerto Rico. MCC had asked Melvin to become director of a CPS camp that was opening near Aibonito. From the beginning, Mary took an intense interest in local culture. She and another CPS wife, Olga Martens, offered sewing classes.

They soon realized that teaching women to sew clothing made almost no dent in their poverty—a poverty precipitated in part by the fact that their husbands too had been drafted by the United States government, leaving the women and children home alone and struggling to make ends meet.[4] What could MCC do?

In visiting with her neighbors and newfound friends, Mary discovered that many women were expert needleworkers. Her ever-creative mind began to whir. Why not encourage these women to do needlepoint rather than machine sewing? Why not provide them with supplies? Why not help them sell their work? She felt certain she could find a market for their finished products. Soon the first MCC-sponsored cottage embroidery industry was off and running in the central highlands of Puerto Rico.

Mary drew paper patterns of both old and new needle-work motifs that she, Olga, and other CPS women distributed along with linen, needles, and thread. On one horseback trip into the mountains, Mary saw examples of an indigenous stitch craft called *collado*. Returning to Aibonito with drawings, she taught the intricate craft to some younger women, encouraging them to reclaim this part of their past.[5]

Initially, the market for the embroidery was limited to U.S. soldiers stationed at a nearby base, other Puerto Ricans, and North American tourists. When an army officer paid two hundred dollars for a linen tablecloth designed by Mary and stitched by one of the workers, Mary and Olga both began to dream of expanding the market to the U.S. mainland.

Then in March 1946, Edna Ruth and J. N. Byler, MCC workers who lived in Mary and Melvin's home while they were gone, visited Puerto Rico. The two CPS women escorted Edna Ruth into a storage room where several shelves held a collection of the fine linen needlework. Would she be willing to take samples back to Akron? When Edna Ruth said yes, Mary made quick sketches of the available designs on graph paper and penciled in suggested retail prices for finished needlework in each pattern.

It was Edna Ruth who nurtured the seeds of the La Plata self-help needlework enterprise into a full-blooming garden. She took Mary's pattern samples to the semiannual meeting of the Lancaster-area Mennonite Women's Sewing Circle. Numerous orders were placed that day. As the 1946 Christmas season approached, the orders poured in, keeping Mary and her needleworkers very busy. For five years the Puerto Rican producers were the sole suppliers for what would become a thriving North American market for various crafts of the world.[6]

In a classic "rest of the story" tale, Edna Ruth's needlework-ordering operation became the Overseas Needlepoint and Crafts Project, which became MCC's SELFHELP Crafts.[7] By 1996 when SELFHELP Crafts changed its name to Ten Thousand Villages, the tiny needlework business had become a multinational, nonprofit trading organization with craft purchases of more than three million dollars a year and net sales approaching eight million dollars a year. A converted shoe factory within easy walking distance of the Akron homes of Edna Ruth Byler and Mary Lauver provided spacious accommodations for the organization's U.S. headquarters.

When Mary and Melvin left Puerto Rico in November 1948, Mary passed the needlework initiative on to other capable hands. Although she supported Edna Ruth's modest basement business, Mary never realized any personal financial gain. For both Edna Ruth and Mary, selling handcrafted needlework was a nonprofit woman-to-woman quest to make life better for their sisters in a developing country. In the way of many service-oriented visionaries, Mary rejoiced to see the project bearing fruit and moved on to other challenges.

While in Puerto Rico, the Lauvers opened their home to a neighborhood child. Their foster son, Louis, was also the only child they would ever have. He was twelve years old when Melvin was ordained at Lititz Mennonite Church on April 20, 1949. Melvin was thirty-six; Mary was thirty-three.

With her usual optimism and warmth, Mary gave herself to the many-layered tasks of being a homemaker, mother, and pastor's wife. She hosted families for Sunday noon meals, taking a special interest in the church's young people. She organized and taught a girls' craft-making club while Melvin led the boys in woodworking. She disliked sitting on the front bench as was expected of preachers' wives in many 1950s Lancaster Mennonite congregations. But Mary Lauver always sat on the front bench because she knew it would help keep the peace.

Although neither Mary nor Melvin received a salary for their unselfish pastoral work, parishioners often gave them supplies such as eggs, meat, and produce. Through the years, they opened dozens of thank-you notes with five- or ten-dollar bills tucked inside. In 1967 the congregation paid for both of them to travel to the Mennonite World Conference in Amsterdam. Many members sustained both their pastor and his wife with words of encouragement and the support of money, prayers, and time.

In his pastorate, Melvin faced a number of difficult situations with a conservative bishop who was concerned about leanings toward liberalism. For example, the bishop reminded Melvin that the *Rules and Discipline*, a written list of rules that guided the collective life of the Lancaster Mennonite Conference during much of the twentieth century, discouraged men from wearing long ties. He asked Melvin to stop wearing a tie to his full-time job as a banker.

Mary refused to let the request frustrate her and urged Melvin not to be discouraged by it either. "Mary was a staunch supporter of me in my situations," says Melvin. "She had a way of encouraging me and keeping my spirits up. I thank God for the wonderful gift of Mary." Melvin Lauver's eyes repeatedly fill with tears and his voice breaks as he talks about the confident and faithful woman who cared deeply for him, who supported him unconditionally, but who also had her own interests outside their home and partnership.

Mary's craft-making, learned from her mother and kept fresh by her own active imagination, brought her recognition in the non-Mennonite Lancaster community as well as the broader Mennonite Church. She had a fine artist's touch that raised her creations, though they sometimes sounded contrived, several notches above kitsch. She also took ceramics classes, eventually buying a kiln that Melvin installed in their basement.

In 1958 a local church women's group invited Mary to come and describe her fondness for making unusual gifts such as painted dishes from heated and reshaped 78-rpm records and miniature shadow boxes with glazed egg shells.[8] On October 31 of that year, the Lancaster *Intelligencer Journal* featured a story about her, complete with a photograph of Mary standing among a collection of craft items. Calling her a "woman with a flair for creating a lot out of very little," the daily morning paper described her craft lectures and noted, "She also is in demand from time to time as a lecturer-demonstrator at church and women's group meetings."[9] Before an audience, Mary handled herself with an intriguing combination of grace and pleasure. It was obvious that she liked what she was doing.

Her leadership and oratorical gifts took center stage as invitations to speak became part of the script of her daily life. With her friend, Beulah Diffenbach, she planned a series of women's retreats that developed into what many Lancaster Mennonites still call the "women's retreat movement." The first such event, held in 1962 at Black Rock Retreat Center near Quarryville, Pennsylvania, attracted more than two hundred women.[10] Between 1962 and 1981, Beulah, Mary, and their steering committee coordinated 118 of these special events for Lancaster Mennonite women. The retreats offered "a time and place where one could go for deep spiritual enrichment and nurture."[11] Women led, nourished, and supported each other. And Mary Lauver, though she was rarely the featured speaker, was almost always present at these gatherings. She served on the steering committee for twenty years.

During these years, Mary also built her own private speaking career around a series of creative handicraft talks. She scheduled presentations in places as diverse as the Elizabethtown Flower Club, the Women's League of Gettysburg College, and Mennonite church sewing circles.[12]

In the late 1960s, as she grew weary of the crafts lecture, Mary developed a candle symbolism talk. "Each of these candles," she would say, "represents a step in our walk with the

Lord. These [shorter] candles are the older folks, whose light has been burning awhile. Tall candles are the young people whose lights have just begun to shine."[13] Then with an array of lighted candles catching a reflection in her glasses, Mary shared her messages of hope and new life in Jesus. In deference to strong Lancaster-area Mennonite feelings about women preaching, she consistently described her symbolic sermon-making as "giving talks." Women from every corner of Lancaster County flocked to the places where she spoke.

One Sunday morning in 1973, Mary discovered an interesting gift on the car seat as she and Melvin headed home after a regular Lititz worship service. Inside a brown paper bag was a container filled with sourdough starter. "It didn't look very ambitious, and I really didn't take it seriously until I had it all over the refrigerator," Mary said.[14] The anonymous giver included a set of instructions, and Mary's high-level creative mind went into gear.

Old-timers told her sourdough starter was made from potatoes, water, and hops. Because she had no easy access to hops, Mary began experimenting, coming up with two things—her own starter recipe and an original inspirational talk, complete with samples of cookies, bread, and rolls to taste, recipes to try, and starter to take home. She gave her sourdough talk 370 times.

In a 1976 interview, Mary explained what the sourdough meant to her. "It's one of the nicest gifts anyone ever gave me. I've just been thrilled by it. The spiritual emphasis of the dough makes it beautiful. You see, the Lord spoke to me about the dough. He said, 'You were given it, not because you merited or earned it, but simply as a gift of love from someone who loves you.'"[15]

A devout and thoughtful woman with expressive eyes and hands, Mary Lauver always attributed the success of her talks to the inspiration of the Holy Spirit.[16] "Teaching the Sunday school classes, giving talks—these activities became much easier because Christ gave me the inspiration, often at night, either when I was asleep or awake, I can't tell," Mary said in one interview. "The Lord put the ideas in my mind."[17]

The last such idea became a series called "Being a Bride Again." From her family treasures, Mary pulled out several old quilts, a wedding dress, a music box, and a collection of stories from her parents' life. Standing among her show-and-tell pieces, she spoke candidly of the joy and pain in any good marriage, the commonsense communication newlyweds needed to consider, and the glorious love passages in the Song of Solomon. From crafts to candles and bread to brides, Mary's symbolic portraits of faithful living changed many Lancaster Mennonite women, inspiring them to go home to their families and everyday work with renewed devotion and strength.

She herself went home to Melvin, to their gracious three-story Akron house. In the easy, light times with her much-loved husband, Mary relaxed. Melvin remembers, "Did you know I used to build canoes? We were so perfectly matched when we went canoeing. She loved it. With Mary and me, everything fit." His are the memories of an old man whose life was defined by the rare gift of more than fifty years with a companion whose natural and settled center connected with his own.

Through all the years of his pastorate at Lititz Mennonite Church, Mary stayed close to Melvin, joining in the celebration of his retirement on November 25, 1979. "We made a great team. Mary loved pastoring with me, but I don't believe she ever wanted to be the pastor."

Indeed, she may never have wished to be pastor, but in partnership with Melvin, Mary did lots of pastoral work, offering words of advice and prayer for dozens of men, women, and children. The Lauvers were known throughout the Lancaster community for their willingness to take troubled people under their wings, sometimes giving entire families a home for several weeks or months as they helped parents recover their dignity and solve their problems. When Melvin agreed to be the first chaplain at the nearby Landis Homes Retirement Community, Mary took a special interest in the women and men who lived there. She frequently brought carloads of residents to her home, where she treated them to an afternoon of fellowship and food.[18]

To Melvin, it is simple: "Mary had a knack for dealing with women." So she did. She made women-to-women connections her life's passion and work. From the Puerto Rico-to-Pennsylvania needlework alliance to the women's retreat movement, Mary found ways to link women with other women.

Compassion, always freely extended to those around her, became both the foundation and composition of Mary Lauver's story. A great light went out when she died at age seventy-three on the first of February 1990. No one missed her more than Melvin Lauver.

Jean K. Shenk

8

Your Father's Mantle

Jean Kraybill Shenk
Mount Joy, Pennsylvania

THE FIRST TIME JEAN KRAYBILL noticed Norman Shenk, he was wearing knickers. They were children at a daytime summer Bible school in Mount Joy, Pennsylvania. "He always knew his verses so well, and I thought that was wonderful," says Jean.[1] Jean came from Mount Joy's rural west side and Norman from its east side to the small town's Mennonite meetinghouse because their respective home congregations—Bossler and Erisman—had no summer Bible school programs. Both Norman's knickers and his careful recitation of Bible memory made a lasting impression on young Jean.

Born in the same calendar year—she on January 12, 1932, and he on December 8, 1932—Jean and Norman spent their formative days on Mennonite family farms in northwestern Lancaster County, in opposite directions but about the same distance from Mount Joy. Margaret and Henry Shenk ran a large cattle and potato operation near Erisman Mennonite Church. Martin and Suie Kraybill farmed a smaller acreage near Bossler.

A charismatic and open man of boundless energy, Jean's father, Martin Kraybill, was never wanting for work. He served on the Bossler ministry team as an unsalaried pastor, following in the footsteps of his father-in-law, Simon E. Garber. He also sold farm seeds among the Amish. "We children couldn't wait for him to come home each evening to hear stories about how he witnessed, how he led people to the Lord," recalls Jean. "That was our life. He always talked about witnessing in such a natural way."

Martin loved to preach, and he traveled throughout Lancaster County, holding itinerant revival meetings in Mennonite churches. His energy and passion earned him many labels: asparagus farmer, evangelist, seed salesman, pastor, winner of souls. To Jean and her siblings, he was Daddy. He was a partner to their more quiet but equally dedicated mother. He was their father, a fascinating man who inspired both his daughters and sons to become educated and pursue their dreams.

Jean and Norman arrived at Lancaster Mennonite School with the class that would graduate in 1950. They were dorm students, but neither remembers for sure when Norman first noticed Jean. Maybe it was during a skating party on Mill Creek. "We had a rule that you couldn't skate together unless you wore gloves," says Jean. "I always made sure I wore gloves, and I remember skating with Norman." Maybe it was soon after a prankster made off with Jean's birthday cake on a cold night in January. Norman's gallant attempt to rescue the cake led to an off-campus pursuit and prompted the dean to issue appropriate penalties. Maybe it was behind a stack of books in the library. "Edna Wenger was the librarian, and she chased us out more than once."

By the time Sister Wenger was ferreting her young charges from behind library stacks, the childhood crush had become a serious mutual attraction. Jean Kraybill married her high school sweetheart on October 18, 1952, a year and a half after graduation. She was twenty; he was nineteen.

Romance quickly yielded to reality. Two weeks after the wedding, the Harrisburg Mennonite Mission, a Manheim district church planting, placed Norman in the lot for minister.[2] When the lot did not fall to him, Jean and Norman planned together to answer his I-W draft classification. They agreed to a two-year assignment at a state mental hospital in Connecticut, leaving their Lancaster home in late November 1952. "Norman and I both worked in the hospital. I was responsible for a ward with as many as fifty disturbed women," Jean recounts. "That stretched me, but it was a good learning experience."

This learning experience was the first of many as the two young people adjusted to what soon became a solid partnership—a partnership in which they each learned that thoughtful listening and shared workloads would be among the keys sustaining their teenage romance. It was also a partnership that caused Norman Shenk to form opinions about many perplexing questions, including the one about women in ministry, "We [he and Jean] have the clear assumption that when the Holy Spirit gives gifts, neither women nor men need to ask permission to minister. We just need to do the work. As we faithfully do the work, we pave the way for the next generation."

Norman completed his I-W alternative service in the fall of 1954. Their first child, Gerald, was already a year old, and the Eastern Board began inquiring whether they would accept an invitation to Ethiopia. Jean explains, "We both came from very mission-supportive families, but neither of us had a college education. There was no money to help us get at least two years of Bible training." The burdens of raising a young family did not permit either Norman or Jean to continue their education. Again, the Eastern Board had an idea. In their conversations with Jean and Norman, they discovered Norman's creative and forward-thinking financial mind. Would he consider working with the treasurer in their home office?

He said yes, and January 1955 marked the beginning of Jean Shenk's twelve-year sojourn as a traditional Lancaster Mennonite housewife and mother. "Norman took the job at a salary of $2,700 a year," Jean recalls. "We moved into the other side of his brother's farmhouse near Erisman, two rooms upstairs, two rooms down. I stayed home. We tried to clothe and feed our family on $200 a month. I figured out how to make one chicken last a whole week."

They planted huge vegetable gardens. They borrowed money to buy land at the corner of Route 230 and what was then Elm Tree Road, working long hours to develop tracts for mobile home sites. The risk exacted sweat and toil, but rent from their mobile village provided extra income, making it possible, among other things, to send each of their three sons— Gerald, Philip, and Steven—to Mennonite schools.

Early in 1963, Norman again found his name put forward for pastoral ministry. This time the lot fell to him, and on February 27 he was ordained to serve his home congregation, Erisman. Jean and Norman Shenk joined the ranks of unsalaried "ordained men and their wives," as Lancaster Mennonites commonly called these caretakers of congregational and spiritual life. From the beginning, Jean understood her role. She had learned well from her grandmother and mother before her.

It was her job to work behind the scenes, to fade into the background of Norman's presence, always there but seldom visible. At Bossler, tradition dictated that the preacher's family did not get involved in teaching Sunday school and other church leadership positions. "No, I was never allowed to teach Sunday school," she says. "I'm not sure my perception was right, but I always thought it was because I was the preacher's daughter. As a teenager I taught summer Bible school at some neighboring churches. But Daddy always said, 'Give the other people at Bossler a chance.'"

Learning from her Bossler experiences, Jean believed that she needed to support Norman while not projecting herself into the church's leadership and decision-making processes. By her actions, Jean expressed this well-learned conviction at Erisman. It was no easy discipline for a woman gifted in advocacy and caretaking; it created a disjunction in how she communicated.

By nature a confident and forthright woman, Jean felt compelled to remove herself from any situation that could be interpreted as the limelight. She constantly reminded herself of her proper place in church life. Norman was the one called to preach, attend church council meetings, plan worship with the other ordained men on the pastoral team, and make public statements about pastoral care questions. Jean was called to be supportive, to help him do his work. It was the way she was taught. It was, in fact, central to Norman's acceptance and success as a leader. It just wasn't easy for this industrious daughter of Martin Kraybill.

Because of their strong personal partnership, Jean, like many other Lancaster Mennonite preachers' wives, participated in much of the pastoral care work. "I went everywhere with Norman—on hospital visits, to counsel those who were hurting, to comfort older people, to funerals and weddings. We also entertained many guests in our home." Together, they bore the burdens of their 200-plus member rural congregation.

The year Norman was ordained, he and Jean also designed and built the house where they still live. There on a triangle of land bordered by Chickies Creek, the old pike from Harrisburg to Lancaster, and the main line of the Pennsylvania Railroad, they raised three lively sons. During these child-rearing years, the Shenk family lived in Belize for six months as Norman took a sabbatical from his work in Eastern Board's home office. Jean also accompanied Norman on some of his administrative visits to overseas mission workers.

As her sons started school and began to mature, Jean became more and more restless. "I do have sort of boundless energy. I was often bored during the day when Norman was at work." Together, Jean and Norman decided she might be happier with a job.

"That first day when I left home and headed for the Mennonite Information Center in Lancaster, I felt so guilty," Jean recounts. "Then I realized there was no one at home, no one who missed or needed me, and no reason to feel guilty. It helped that Norman believed we were doing the right thing." For the next fifteen years, this job kept Jean Shenk whole. She had a natural forum for sharing her faith.

The Mennonite Information Center gave various mission-minded Mennonites such as Jean Shenk a platform for interpreting Anabaptist beliefs. They were called on to share their faith with the growing number of visitors who flocked to Lancaster County to see the Amish. Lancaster-area Mennonites eagerly supported this unique opportunity to provide information services while also giving witness to their Christian faith.

Several years after opening a brochure and map center, the supporting board of the Mennonite Information Center decided to build a reproduction of the Old Testament Hebrew tabernacle on the grounds. Planning the unusual structure during a proliferation of Amish-related attractions and theme parks, Lancaster Mennonites hoped the Tabernacle would leave their guests with more meaningful Amish-area memories. For Jean it was an ideal job, bringing renewed sense of purpose. She researched and studied Old and New Testaments to better answer the many questions visitors posed after experiencing the Tabernacle presentation. Like her father before her, she reveled in the chance to talk about Jesus and the meaning of life.

As she traveled with Norman, Jean's horizons expanded. She observed the many-faceted lives of women in other cultures, comparing their stories with her own. "When Norman and I traveled to Asia and Africa, I was impressed with the oppression of the women," she says. "In Bangladesh, it was especially depressing. Women seldom appeared in the outside world and then only when garbed in the *burkqa*, a black covering from head to foot. From there we traveled to Tanzania, where women had freedom compared to Bangladesh. I asked myself—why the difference? The answer came that Jesus is in Tanzania. Jesus is there and Jesus came to set the captive free. And isn't it true here in our country that where Jesus is, there is liberty and freedom?"[3]

Cast in the context of Jean's personal struggle with public ministry, her questions raised interesting points of concern for both Norman and Jean. Where could she find fulfillment? How might she use her gifts? What was the right thing to do?

Two circumstances propelled Jean from the Mennonite Information Center into the next stage of her ministry. A neighbor in the Erisman community developed cancer and faced the agony of slowly letting go. "Members of our church took turns to stay with her," says Jean. "I remember I was a wreck. It was so hard for me to be with this woman who was dying."

Around the same time, a young woman in the Erisman congregation suffered through a severe mental dissociation. "I felt so helpless. These two instances triggered me to get some training, some help. I heard Sam Thomas [a local Mennonite pastor] talk about a program at Lancaster General Hospital (LGH) called Clinical Pastoral Education (CPE). Winters at the Information Center were always slow, so I decided to apply."

In Jean's second week of classes, she was scheduled to be the nighttime on-call chaplain at LGH. The hospital had three deaths, which made the evening unforgettable. "The first two families had so much pain and so little support," Jean recounts. "I went back to my room and said, 'Lord, I cannot handle this. You have to give me something to say.' I opened my Bible to Psalm 27:13-14 and read, 'I am still confident of this: I will see the goodness of the Lord in the land of the living. Wait for the Lord; be strong and take heart and wait for the Lord'" (NIV).

The beeper went off again. This time Jean felt much less anxious. She was able to give comfort to a grieving family, walking with them through the first steps of their new reality. She would soon begin to discern a niche for her gifts.

Two more units of clinical work at LGH and one at Philhaven Hospital expanded her knowledge of the healing arts. "During the course at Philhaven, John Lederach was guiding the class through a genogram," Jean says. "I was shocked when he said, 'Jean, I think your father's mantle is on your shoulders.' I just did not feel it would be safe to admit that."

In the privacy of her heart, Jean wondered if her ministry might be a calling, but publicly she concentrated on the work at hand. People like Paul M. Miller, Philhaven's CPE supervisor, and Ken Bernette, supervisor of the same program at LGH, affirmed and encouraged her gifts.

As her training continued, Jean began to notice an unexpected truth. Members of Amish and Mennonite churches who were admitted to the hospital rarely received ongoing regular visits from their pastors. Jean understood. She was the wife of an unsalaried pastor, and she knew how difficult it was for someone with a full-time job outside the congregation to provide for the pastoral needs of parishioners.

She dared to dream. Would her people, the Lancaster Mennonite Conference, support her to do this work? Could she be a chaplain for Anabaptist-related people? She wrote to the Bishop Board. After outlining her vision, Jean penned this closing paragraph, "I would enjoy being accountable to someone, giving a report of patients visited and a summary of significant contacts. I have sensed the need for a visitation ministry to Mennonite hospital patients and I have felt a call for this work. I am eager for your response."[4]

On September 16, 1985, the thirty-seven bishops present at their regular monthly meeting considered Jean's request. In keeping with their protocol, they hesitated to make any quick decisions about the troublesome question of women doing public ministry. They agreed, however, to take her inquiry under advisement: "In view of the hospital visiting concern presented by Jean K. Shenk, it was recommended that the Leadership Council give consideration to her letter."[5]

This relatively nonthreatening first step generated some unwanted heat. One bishop approached Jean directly and said, "Well, maybe you've finally found a ministry need that you could fill. But I want you to know you'll never get it." It was an unsettling time for Jean. She had wanted to work with overworked pastors, not threaten them. She meant to make their jobs easier and to give their people an extra layer of support during times of despair and loss.

It was Norman's turn to support his wife's ministry. He describes how and why he stood with Jean by telling a story from his childhood. "Some of my siblings were great singers. My mother thought I didn't have an ear for music, and it used to really frustrate me. Then I got a mouth organ for Christmas. I made up mind I would learn to play, and I would be good at it." He succeeded, and in spite of his mother's fears, was elected song-leader at Erisman when he was only sixteen.

Norman goes on to explain how his childhood experience connects to the narrative of Jean's call: "I don't know if you would call such determination a vice or a virtue. But we both have it. When someone tells either one of us that we will never do something, that's just what we need. We will try very hard to prove them wrong."

The Leadership Council of the Bishop Board considered Jean's request for almost a year. On June 19, 1986, they gave a report and recommendation to thirty-five gathered bishops.

"Correspondence was received concerning supplementary visits in the Lancaster area hospitals and the availability of Jean Shenk to serve. . . . It was recommended that the Board support a plan for meeting this need and that Howard Witmer explore with his district ministry the forming of a support and accountability group to work with Jean Shenk in this ministry."[6]

So the Mennonite Chaplaincy Advisory Committee was created, and in December 1986 the Bishop Board sent a letter of clarification to Lancaster Conference congregations: "Our Board of Bishops has agreed to commission Jean K. Shenk as a hospital chaplain for visitation to Mennonite patients in the Lancaster area hospitals. This visitation program will supplement the good pastoral care given by our pastors and is not intended to replace their ministry."[7]

Every Monday, Wednesday, and Friday, Jean Kraybill Shenk makes her rounds of the three Lancaster hospitals— LGH, St. Joseph's, and Community. She claims Isaiah 40:1 as her directive, "These are my people. Comfort them for me" (NIV). When she arrives at each hospital, she checks the computer bank to see who has been admitted from Anabaptist-related groups, "The computer listing tells me what church affiliation they have," she explains.

She also takes a second look at those patients who claim no church family. "I am always surprised by how many have Amish or Mennonite connections." Often these are people who were hurt by the church. Gently she hears their stories—sometimes painful tales of abuse, neglect, and oppression. "One question my father often asked people was, 'Where do you worship?' I find that's not as threatening as saying, 'Do you know Jesus?' which I do not ask these patients." Instead she listens.

One such encounter led Jean to minister to a dying woman who had left her abusive husband many years earlier. The resulting divorce, initiated by her husband, prompted a local Mennonite congregation to excommunicate not only Marie (not her real name), but also her parents after she asked them for help with her two young children. Marie was surprised when Jean, who wears her hair up with a traditional Mennonite covering, offered sympathy and indicated it was safe to share her story.

The Lancaster Mennonite Conference, Jean told her, had since moved past its rejection of those affected by divorce. Many of its congregations did their best to be compassionate toward those touched by such pain. "I told her that the church was ready to listen to stories of abuse from women who have been hurt and victimized," Jean says. "All I could say was I was so sorry the church was not there to support her."

Marie did not recover from her illness. Her two sons joined the LGH staff chaplain for a graveside service. After hearing their story of rejection from the church, the chaplain, who was not Mennonite, decided to offer a statement of apology. It was a healing moment for two successful, Lancaster-area men who had been raised outside a church tradition, not by choice but by decree. The chaplain later approached Jean, and through her advocacy, a local Mennonite bishop also sent a letter of apology to the sons. Ministering to Marie and advocating for her sons had given Jean Shenk another opportunity to make a difference.

Making a difference is the essence of her work. As a hospital chaplain, Jean comforts the bereaved, prays for the sick, and shares God's love through her presence. "But I'm not a hospital staffperson," Jean clarifies. From the beginning, Jean has seen her ministry as a link in the Anabaptist congregational network. She does not attempt to care for individual patients in the same way their pastors care for them. She simply hopes to alleviate the pastor's workload with advocacy, intervention, and the follow-up visits that most pastors, whether or not they receive a salary, find difficult to make.

Her consistent presence in the three Lancaster hospitals affords her an inside track and a rapport with staff that often makes small details of human comfort more accessible to patients. "Our people are somewhat withdrawn and conditioned not to bother the nurses. Sometimes, especially when they're sick, they just don't know how to ask for little comforts. I am their advocate. If the sun shines in their eyes, I pull the blinds and tell them it's fine to ask someone to open the curtains later. Every patient needs an advocate." Whether she's explaining to a doctor why an Amish woman wishes to wear her head covering into surgery or asking a psychiatrist to place a homeless woman with Mennonite connections in a Mennonite-related institution, Jean faces a constant sea of need.

Her ministry has been endorsed by official action of the Bishop Board, but the question, "Could individual pastors do the work just as well?" lingers around the edges. On November 22, 1992, she was given credentials when the Erisman congregation licensed her as a deaconess assigned to hospital chaplaincy work. Jean depends on designated freewill gifts channeled through the Lancaster Mennonite Conference treasury. She lives with the knowledge that her financial remuneration will stop if the specific gifts disappear.

The sea of need and the lingering questions sometimes weigh heavily on her mind. "This is not easy work. I do bring the burdens of my day home. I am so thankful for my dear Norman. He is such a good listener."

She also takes courage from her sons. "I do a report to my chaplaincy support group once a month. This last time I sent the report to all three of my sons by e-mail," Jean recounts. "Gerald, who is on the staff at Eastern Mennonite Seminary, asked if I would like to come down and describe my work at the seminary." There is awe in Jean Shenk's voice. She, a woman who never found money or time to get a college degree, was being asked to address Mennonite seminarians. "What a great honor."

Jean says her sons have been very supportive of her work. "Steve just said something the other day about how I comfort people. He said, 'Well, Mother, it's something you do really well.' That was a compliment. When it comes from your son, it means a lot."

For Jean, the most important part of her work has been sharing her faith—wearing, as it were, her father's mantle. "My greatest joys have come when I've been able to lead someone to faith in Jesus, when I've been able to offer them a lasting hope." Like her father before her, Jean loves to tell the stories of witnessing, of watching people's lives change when they meet Jesus. She often refers new Christians to local Mennonite pastors, depending on them to assist her in the all-important follow-up calls and visits.

As she and Norman recently passed age sixty-five, they turned with energy and a certain youthful vitality to the next stage of their lives. On Wednesday, December 31, 1997, Norman retired from Eastern Mennonite Missions after forty-three years of service. Earlier, he also resigned from the pastoral team at Erisman.

Jean, who continues her chaplaincy work, comments, "We love the church. I'm sure we will always be involved." In fact, Norman has already agreed to volunteer four days a week at Eastern Mennonite Missions (formerly Eastern Board).

Together, these two Lancaster Mennonite Conference leaders will continue to demonstrate, with their human hands and voices, the transcendent love of God.

Lena Brown

An Ordinary Country Girl

Lena Horning Brown
Grantham, Pennsylvania

THE 1890S GREAT AWAKENING spread its influence far into the twentieth-century Lancaster Conference experience. After rapid spurts of early growth, the congregations and mission programs that came out of the revival movement settled into a more even growth pattern.

The 1920s brought affluence and wealth. The 1930s cast the clouds of the Great Depression over businesses, farmland, and homesteads. Although some Lancaster Mennonites became rich during the "Roaring '20s," flaunting wealth was never considered appropriate. Most remained devoutly frugal. When the stock market crashed in 1929, these careful farmers and financiers pulled more tightly into themselves. Some Mennonites lost money. Many became more convinced than ever that frugality and spareness were essential Christian virtues.

This consciousness generated what appear to be opposite reactions. On the one hand, the Lancaster Mennonite Conference and its leaders withdrew into themselves. Power became entrenched in the rapidly expanding Bishop Board. In their October 1932 meeting, the Bishop Board re-emphasized previous statements prohibiting divorce, bathing beaches, swimming pools, and community shows. They also noted the "present depression" and instructed the Eastern Board to raise money and distribute funds to members of their churches with needs.[1]

On the other hand, the Bishop Board and the Eastern Board entered into a partnership that swung wide the gates to cross-cultural experience and forever realigned the shapes of the conference. On July 14, 1930, the Bishop Board decided to "take several months to further consider the matter of opening a mission in Africa." On October 1, 1930, they unanimously favored "the starting of a Mission in Africa under the Eastern Mennonite Board of Missions and Charities."

Three years later, when Lena Horning was only eight months old, Elam Stauffer and Orie Miller were on their way to scout the land and open a mission somewhere in East Africa. They were plainly dressed Lancaster Mennonites seeking to settle on a different continent because they took Christ's word seriously: "Go ye therefore, and teach all nations, baptizing them in the name of the Father, and of the Son, and of the Holy Ghost" (Matt. 28:19).

These opposing impulses—to go into all the world and to withdraw into themselves—defined both experience and understanding for many children born into Lancaster Mennonite homes between 1930 and 1950. Lena Horning was such a child. Born to Harvey B. and Nancy Horning of Denver, Pennsylvania, on March 6, 1933, Lena was raised with a high sense of personal frugality and separateness from the world. She also heard mission workers on furlough describe the beauty and extravagance, the frightening differences, and the comforting similarities of the diverse peoples with whom they lived and worked.

When Lena was ten years old, the Bowmansville congregation, where her father served as deacon, organized its youth group into a Christian Worker Band. The goal was to "give purposeful activity to the young people and to give a Christian testimony to the unsaved."[2] Because this farm congregation was in the same bishop district as the city mission churches in Reading, many young people in the Christian Worker Band taught Sunday school or summer Bible school in downtown Reading. Lena, who still wears her soft gray hair gathered under a modest early 1950s Lancaster Mennonite covering, worked in two different churches as a teenager.

On the surface, Lena Horning's upbringing prepared her to be a simple Mennonite farm woman likely to stay in Lancaster County all her life, a woman at peace with the movement of families, fields, and flowers. But directly beneath the surface was another narrative. "I begged to go to high school because I was sure I wanted to be a teacher," Lena recounts. "It was not common for Bowmansville Mennonite girls to finish high school, but my parents never tried to stop me. They were always so affirming."[3]

She graduated with Lancaster Mennonite School's class of 1952 and went on to Eastern Mennonite College, where she earned a degree in elementary education. When the doors to broader knowledge opened, she walked through them. She also returned to her rural home community, teaching school and taking part in church life in the Bowmansville area for seven years.

Sally Hurst, the wife of the pastor at South Seventh Street Mennonite Church in Reading, recognized something special in Lena's manner of life and testimony. It was she who suggested Lena's name to the Eastern Board as a possible candidate for overseas mission work. After an exploratory interview in 1960 with Paul N. Kraybill, Lena chose to stay home two more years to finish paying off a college loan from her parents. By the year she turned twenty-nine, Lena was ready. She agreed to go to Somalia.

Less than a month before her scheduled departure, shocking news arrived at Eastern Board Salunga headquarters. Harold Stauffer from the Somalia mission in Mogadishu reported that co-worker Merlin Grove had been stabbed to death on July 16, 1962. Merlin's wife Dorothy was badly wounded. Harold, who came to their rescue, escaped only by outrunning the assailant, which gave the mission time to secure the premises.[4]

The terrible news shook both Eastern Board and the Somalia mission to the core. What had gone wrong? Keenly aware of pressures to outlaw Christian witness because of Somalia's predominantly Muslim culture, the Mennonite mission tried to heed the government's changing edicts. They had closed their schools several months before the attack, but when permission came to reopen, they did so, inflaming the passions of an isolated extremist. Merlin was killed while registering students. Dorothy slowly recovered from her physical wounds. Words of sympathy poured in from the Somali people. The prime minister personally expressed his regrets and appealed to the Mennonites to stay. Most of the workers stayed.[5]

Paul Kraybill asked Lena, "Do you still want to go?" Convinced of God's call, she said yes, knowing that she would be in the south of Somalia and somewhat removed from the capital city's tensions. In early August, she boarded a plane in New York and flew to Mogadishu on a roundabout route by way of London, Khartoum, and Nairobi.

As Lena disembarked the airplane in Mogadishu, she stepped into the equatorial winds of a steaming seaside city. "I remember it was hot and noisy, but I also had a spirit of eagerness and excitement, of wanting to learn from this very different culture," she says. Within days, she traveled overland to the Mennonite mission and the Jamama Mission School in southern Somalia, leaving the seasoned workers to their more immediate concerns and sadness.

"When I was in Somalia [1962-1966], it was a good time to be there. The Grove tragedy moved people to support Mennonites, and our mission was well thought of. We had lots of freedom." This was prior to later difficulties, Lena shares—difficulties including intense impoverishment and numerous outbreaks of war.

In 1967 Eastern Board transferred Lena to Nairobi, Kenya, where she became one of the first teachers at the brand-new Mennonite missionary boarding school, Rosslyn Academy. Centrally located so missionary parents working in Ethiopia, Tanzania, and Somalia could send their children to the academy, Rosslyn came to define an interesting chapter in Lancaster Mennonite mission history. Lena was a central figure in the early years of that story.

"Going away to boarding school worked for some children, but for others it just did not work," Lena remembers. Missionary parents agonized over the need to send their children away for months at a time. Some children thrived, but others suffered. "I was one of the classroom teachers. I know the house parents had more to deal with than we did because the evenings were the hardest times for the little ones."

While living in Nairobi, Lena attended a local Baptist church. A California librarian named Mike Brown also attended the church. Mike, who was in Kenya with Mennonite Central Committee's Teachers Abroad Program (TAP), volunteered to catalog the new boarding school's library.

"We don't remember when we first saw each other," says Lena now. They were two very different people. Lena was a country girl from Bowmansville; Mike was a small-town boy from Chino, on the western edge of California's San Bernardino County. As a child, she went to Mennonite worship services Sunday morning and evening, sometimes afternoons as well; he occasionally attended a Baptist Sunday school. As a young adult, she fully embraced the Mennonite faith, wearing distinctive clothing and upholding the church's doctrines and standards; he did not encounter Anabaptist teachings until he began attending a small Brethren in Christ church as a high school junior.

From her earliest memories, Lena knew about and accepted the Anabaptist-Mennonite objection to all forms of violence, usually called nonresistance by the leaders and preachers at churches like Bowmansville. Mike chose TAP after becoming convinced of the peace position, making it impossible for him to join the military at the height of the Vietnam War.

Sometime during their uneventful acquaintance in Nairobi, they noticed each other. When Mike, who is nine years younger than Lena, wrote a letter after his return to the States in 1969, the first sparks of romance were lit. Through correspondence they overcame differences in age, culture, and religion to forge a friendship and lay the foundation for what would become a life together.

Lena came home in August 1970 determined to finish her master's degree in education before making any other major life decisions. After completing the degree at Millersville (Pa.) State College, she married Mike on February 6, 1971, in the comfortable surroundings of Bowmansville Mennonite Church. They moved to California.

On April 5, 1972, Lena, who had just turned thirty-nine, gave birth to their son Lowell. "Mike had done his undergraduate work at Upland College, and the former librarian at Upland invited Mike to consider a vacancy at Messiah. We decided to come back east." In 1973 they packed their VW Bug and set out on a cross-country trip that would bring Lena back to within an hour's drive of the Bowmansville farm where she grew up.

Perched on a hill above the crossroads hamlet of Grantham, Pennsylvania, Messiah College connected the Brown family to the local Brethren in Christ community. "We thought we'd like to attend a church where we could also develop connections and friendships with people other than the college community," Lena explains. They found Slate Hill Mennonite Church, and the first page of an altogether new chapter in Lena Brown's life was written.

A few years after Lena and Mike joined the church, Slate Hill members began to discuss sponsoring a Vietnamese refugee family. Lena agreed to be secretary for the project, and the Kanty San family of six moved to Grantham in October 1975. A full-time mother to Lowell, Lena willingly opened herself and their home to the small group of people forced to flee their homeland in the final hours of a horrible war.

"In those first days, it always seemed the stories were too painful to recall," she says. "They lived with us for about a week and a half until we found a house for them. Most of the family just wanted to begin a new life and forget about the old."

Accustomed to the lush tropical lowlands of Vietnam, the San family adjusted slowly to the climate and complexities of American life. Lena, along with other folks at Slate Hill, was there to help them make the necessary transitions. She found doctors, furniture, food stores, jobs, schools, and English classes. She sat nearby and watched as they worked through immigration red tape in the capital city of Harrisburg, twelve miles north of Grantham. She answered their questions and prayed for their safety and security.

Often with baby Miriam, adopted in March 1978, perched on her hip, Lena became a familiar figure in the community as she advocated for the various needs of her Vietnamese friends. Recognizing that both the church and those coming to America were enriched by this shared bond, the Slate Hill church council suggested sponsoring additional Asian refugees.[6] So began Lena Brown's Lao ministry.

The first Lao family, who also lived with Lena and Mike until a nearby apartment was ready, came to Grantham in October 1979. The Slate Hill congregation gave full sponsorship to two Vietnamese and seven Lao families, as well as partial support to a number of other families. Other local churches also operated refugee programs, creating a vibrant Lao community in and around Harrisburg. Eventually, the more settled family members and friends cared for new arrivals.

But everyone, it seemed, turned to Lena for help with the day-to-day details of American life. She drove pregnant mothers to the hospital, young men to drivers' license offices, and people of all ages to job interviews. One day she accompanied a young woman to the Dauphin County courthouse to file for a marriage license. Because the groom's Florida paperwork was incomplete, the normally easy half-hour process turned into an afternoon of waiting in one line after another to see a collection of officials. Lena's patience with the bureaucracy of government helped to transform what could have been an upsetting experience for the Lao woman into a successful trip. "I learned that they also serve who sit and wait," says Lena.[7]

Lena's gifts of time to people like the young woman, whose power was limited by circumstances, did not escape the notice of her church. "Whenever a new family came, I made a list of needs—beds, a table, chairs, cookware. People always pitched in. The church treasurer gave money gladly. A prayer support group of eight couples met regularly to pray with me for the Lao work. Anytime I had a tough problem, I knew I could turn to one of them for advice and counsel."

The Slate Hill congregation also interacted with the Lao families during worship services. From June 1981 until the early 1990s, a volunteer regularly drove a bus to Harrisburg to pick up those who wished to participate in a Mennonite church. "That part has not been easy," admits Lena. "For some years now, we've had a separate Lao fellowship. I've always felt we need to find more ways to incorporate the Lao language into our English services. Many of the teenagers and young families come to the English service. They read Scripture in Lao or English if they want, sing in the Lao language, or work as greeters and ushers."

Lena's focused ministry and vision gradually assimilated her Lao friends into the local environs and also attracted the attention of the greater Harrisburg community. On July 14, 1986, the Rotary Club of Harrisburg honored her with a "Service Above Self Award." They invited Lena and Mike to a luncheon where they presented a bronze plaque of recognition, a book called *Freedom's Holy Light*, and a one thousand-dollar check for a charity of her choice. "We gave five hundred dollars to the Slate Hill Lao ministry and five hundred dollars to Catholic Charities, the agency that nominated me for the award."

Lena's generous volunteer service, the Rotary Club said, symbolized what the American Statue of Liberty stands for—"a light to the homeless, the poor, the tired, and those yearning to be free."[8] A local newscast reported the event, and the local newspaper printed a feature story. Ever a modest person, Lena hesitates to receive congratulations. "I wasn't looking for honors. I was just doing the work God called me to do."

During a 1986 congregational meeting at Slate Hill, Ruth Musselman stood up and spoke of Lena's commitment to the Lao work. "Why don't we make Lena a deacon?" she asked. Lena was taken aback at first, but then she remembered her father, a deacon at Bowmansville Mennonite Church from 1940-1981.

"Some of his work was very different from what I had been doing. He was the troubleshooter for disciplinary problems and the treasurer of what we called the deacon fund, money set aside for mutual aid. Then I remembered the many times I had gone with him to deliver groceries to needy families. I remembered what a good listener he was. I thought about his depth and quiet strength." Lena realized that she was indeed her father's daughter and that she could and had been doing the work of a deacon.

With the encouragement of her pastor, Samuel Troyer, Lena agreed to enter into a process leading to a deaconess license. In April 1986, Slate Hill sent a letter to the Lancaster Conference Bishop Board, asking for permission to license Lena. Although many more requests would follow in the next few years, no such official request for credentialing a woman had ever come before this body of leaders. The inquiry was noted in the Board's April minutes, without comment, as "deaconess for Slate Hill, PA." The May 19 minutes highlighted a small revision to the April minutes—a note clarifying that the request should have read "deaconess (license) for Slate Hill, PA."

Licensing women for leadership was not an entirely new thought for the Bishop Board. Beginning as early as January 1986, the Board, which had grown to include more than thirty men, and a task force organized by the Board of Congregational Resources engaged in a few preliminary conversations about women in ministry. On February 20, 1986, the Task Force on Women in Church and Family, which had been working since May 1982, joined the bishops and two invited guest speakers for a daylong session titled "Men and Women in Ministry."

Sanford G. Shetler, a conservative historian and theologian from Johnstown, Pennsylvania, expounded at length on the question, "Does the New Testament Support the Ordination of Women?" His conclusion was an unequivocal "no." Willard Swartley, a professor at Associated Mennonite Biblical Seminaries, Elkhart, Indiana, took exception with Sanford's conclusion, citing various texts and New Testament teachings that relate directly to Jesus and other church leaders identifying women in ministry. A planned time of open discussion had to be shelved for lack of time. At the end of the day, however, the secretary noted that the bishops would "consider preparing guidelines for choosing and authorizing the offices of deaconess and elders." No action was taken.[9]

Meanwhile, Samuel Troyer continued to advocate for a license for Lena by speaking with John Kraybill, the bishop of the Harrisburg district. The congregation agreed that Lena deserved and needed affirmation for her Lao work. They also decided she would have more "impact in dealing with secular authorities if she represented an official position of the church," according to a written history of the church.[10] Sometime during that eventful summer of 1986, Samuel suggested Lena should be called to serve the entire congregation, not only the Lao fellowship. Again, the congregation agreed.

John Kraybill and Samuel Troyer decided to take action. They scheduled a service of licensing for January 4, 1987. The Bishop Board did not openly object, and Lena Brown became the first woman in the Lancaster Mennonite Conference to receive credentials for pastoral ministry. "I didn't think about blazing a trail," Lena says now. "I just thought about getting back to work. We were preparing for a new family's arrival."

Two months later, the Bishop Board again took up the issue of women in ministry at its monthly meeting. They received a written report on the subject of women's roles, established a deaconess study committee, and read a letter of clarification "in the recent licensing of a deaconess." By official action, the bishops proposed "to recognize her at Conference Assembly and inform her she does not have voting privileges."[11]

The recognition without rights was a giant step for the Bishop Board, though it was a small step for Lena Horning Brown. As she had been doing for more than twelve years, she went back to her work, faithfully providing aid to those who might otherwise be forced to deal alone with a confusing new world. After several more years of debate and study, the Bishop Board extended voting rights to Lena and the subsequently licensed deaconesses at their Spring 1991 assembly.[12]

The significance of being the first woman with credentials has seeped like a slow-falling rain into Lena's consciousness. In 1987 she told an interviewer, "I'm not a pioneer woman."[13] In 1998 she said, "Perhaps I can pioneer a little longer."[14] The eleven years that passed between those two comments brought great change to her life, which she says is a testimony to God's grace. She moved from deaconess to associate pastor. She went from teaching Sunday school to preaching Sunday morning sermons. She even consented to enter a process leading to ordination.

"I have always felt that being vocal and pushy about my call does more harm than good," says Lena. "But I also think as an older woman I may be more acceptable to conference leaders. I'm willing to be first if it opens doors for others."

In February 1998, the Slate Hill elder team composed a letter to the Bishop Board, requesting full ordination for Lena Brown. The team described Lena's gifts and the congregational process leading to the petition. More than ten years had passed since the bishops had completed their deaconess study, and once again they were immersed in an extended period of discussion about women in ministry. The task force's successor, a group called the Women in Leadership Subcommittee (WILS), had been advocating for women. Their persistent work brought open discussion about women in leadership into the public sphere of Lancaster Mennonite life.

The bishops gathered into themselves, taking the matter under advisement and producing a statement on women in leadership. Letters, seminars, studies, and revised versions of the statement filled the halls of the Lancaster Conference offices at 2160 Lincoln Highway East. In addition to Slate Hill's inquiry about Lena Brown, several other Lancaster Conference congregations requested permission to ordain women leaders in their churches (see Author's Preface). The bishops asked for more time.

Although several of the other congregations spoke actively and openly, hoping for a quick resolution to the question, Slate Hill agreed to wait as the process worked itself out. "It's obvious to me that there are two poles of opinion about women in leadership," says Lena. "I will do the work whether or not I am ordained. But to tell you the truth, sometimes I'm afraid they'll spend so much time studying the issue that I'll be retired before they make a decision." These three sentences capture the essence of Lena Brown. She respects those who don't agree with her; she does the work; she hopes to be ordained.

"It amazes me to be in this spot at this time. After all, I'm just an ordinary Mennonite country girl. At first when Roger [Steffy, lead pastor at Slate Hill] asked me to take a regular turn preaching, I wasn't sure. But you know, preaching is very close to teaching. I find I really enjoy preparing sermons. Right now I'm working on one about Jesus feeding the four thousand. What do you say about such a familiar story? Every time when I'm working on a sermon, I ask myself those kinds of questions, and every time I discover something new."

Adjustments and changes are not strangers to Lena Brown. In the fall of 1997, she discovered a lump on one of her breasts. In a traumatic set of circumstances leading up to Christmas, her breast was removed. "It was different to be the one getting care from the church," she recollects. "Those were not easy days."

Several months later, on the Sunday before Valentine's Day, Lena was recovering rapidly and back in a more familiar role—standing in the pulpit at Slate Hill. In a modified Pennsylvania Dutch accent, her carefully chosen words painted the scenes of an extraordinary story of love, the love Leah felt for her jilted husband, Jacob. "Leah could have been very bitter toward God for putting her in such a difficult situation," Lena said in that sermon. "Sometimes love demands hard things. Sometimes love is tough."[15]

As always, Lena Brown decided to go on with the work. She would leave the theorizing and opinion making to others. She only hoped they wouldn't wait too long.

Mattie Cooper Nikiema

10

Where the Word of God Was Taught, People Believed

Mattie Cooper Nikiema
Philadelphia, Pennsylvania

WHEN MATTIE COOPER'S great-grandfather, Richmond Jackson, finally was a free man at the end of the Civil War, he left rural Burke County, Georgia, to find his little sister. She lived downriver, he had been told, in the port city of Savannah. Hiking south through east-central Georgia, he followed the roads, towns, and trails between the Ogeechee and Savannah Rivers, stopping along the way to rest or exchange work for food. The hundred miles passed quickly under his young feet.

Richmond found his sister. Gently, he put her on his shoulders and carried her all the way back to his sharecropper home where he raised her alongside his own children, one of whom became Mattie's grandmother, Minnie. "Grandpop Jackson was married three times. He outlived each of his wives," says Mattie. "Only as an adult did I begin to figure out all the different ways my great-aunts and great-uncles were related to each other. The Jackson family still has regular reunions. This summer [1998] they're coming to Philadelphia."[1]

Minnie, whose birth date was unknown, inherited both her father's compassion and his will to succeed. "She was a very

159

spiritual, very down-to-earth person. Most of the things I know today in the way of homespun wisdom and idioms and proverbs, I learned from my grandmother," says Mattie. "She has been my role model."

Mattie Cooper's grandmother was an exceptionally determined and gifted person. She graduated from high school sometime in the early 1900s, a young black woman in the heart of the divided black and white South. She taught school. She waited to marry until she was twenty-eight years old. Then, she raised her family alone when her husband died young, leaving her with a one-week-old baby and four other children under the age of seven.

Mattie's mother, Easter Jackson, was the second of those five children. It was Easter who left Burke County for Philadelphia, joining the mass exodus of people who left the rural South at the height of segregation, hoping to escape the suffocating Jim Crow laws. Mattie, born September 18, 1937, stayed behind to live with her grandmother on the Jackson family farm. "We would come to Philadelphia to visit my mother and my aunt who also lived here. We went to Savannah and other places around Georgia where my grandmother's relatives were. We liked to travel."

These strong country folks were Mattie Cooper's people—women and men of faith, with ordinary dreams and simple lives. They were also people with extraordinary courage, who made decisions that improved not only their own circumstances, but also the circumstances of their children and children's children.

When Mattie was twelve, she moved north to join her mother and two younger half brothers. A year or so after Mattie settled in Philadelphia, two plainly dressed Mennonite women knocked on the front door of Easter Jackson's house. "It was Alma Ruth and Emma Rudy, and they were looking for the people who had lived in our house before us. So, of course, they invited us to come to Diamond Street church. I remember very clearly that they said, 'Just come as you are. You don't have to dress up.'

"The next Sunday my mother went to investigate. She came back, saying, 'Yes, indeed, the people dressed very simply.' You see, we had always been regular church attenders, members of the Methodist faith. But if you didn't have a certain style of attire at the Methodist church in our neighborhood, you felt out of place. We were poor. So many a Sunday we didn't go because we didn't have proper clothes."

Easter Jackson and her three children—Mattie Cooper, Raymond, and William Jackson—began attending the Mennonite mission, a few hops and skips along the sidewalk from their 19th Street home to 1814 West Diamond Street. In February 1952, Mattie and her mother attended their first membership instruction class. Two months later, Emma Rudy noted she had spent the day "making dresses for Mrs. Jackson and Mattie." Then on Sunday morning, April 27, they put on the plain attire of Lancaster Mennonites and walked to church, where they were baptized and received into membership.[2] The younger Jackson boys joined Diamond Street in the early 1960s.[3]

The Cooper-Jackson family stayed at Diamond Street for many reasons. They loved Alma and Emma, the two women who founded the work after originally coming to the city to serve the nearby Philadelphia Home Mission. Mattie, her mother, and later both of her brothers discovered their own convictions fit easily into the revival language and spiritual underpinnings of the 1940s Mennonite way. They cherished the Bible preaching and teaching. They resonated with the gospel hymns and come-to-Jesus sermons that Lancaster Mennonites had learned from Methodist revival ministers a half-century earlier. In matters of faith and Bible teaching, they felt at home.

The language about dress and style of life was a different matter. It was one thing to wear simple clothing; it was quite another to change wardrobes after being received into church membership. In the context of this caring community, however, they were even willing to make those adjustments. "I started wearing a covering and cape dress within six months after we first went to Diamond Street," says Mattie. "You see, we had community there. When I talk about 'we' as a group at Diamond Street, I mean my brothers and me; the Allen girls, Margaret, Barbara, and Doris; and their three brothers. And there were many others."

The Mennonite mission's humble corner row house was indeed a community-centered building. It had a third-floor apartment where the two sister workers lived for nineteen years, 1942-1961. It had a second-floor apartment where a stream of Lancaster Mennonite couples stayed while the men served as short-term pastors, often on their way to mission assignments elsewhere. The building's main floor had been remodeled to resemble the interior of a 1940s Lancaster Mennonite meetinghouse, complete with pews, a preacher's table, and two pulpit chairs. Wrapped around the walls in large, block letters were the following excerpts from Scripture: "O, Come Let Us Worship the Lord," "The Wages of Sin Is Death," and "Believe on the Lord Jesus Christ and Thou Shalt Be Saved."[4]

When Mattie's family came to Diamond Street, the first long-term pastor and his wife, Luke and Miriam Stoltzfus, had been there less than a year. Their church and home was near the heart of a dynamic urban community. Shops sold everything from candy and groceries to hair-care items, radios, and even newfangled televisions. Children filled the streets with laughter, flocking to hear Alma and Emma tell their flannelgraph Bible stories and sing from illustrated song sheets. Mattie, the Allen girls, and numerous other neighborhood young people soon became intimately involved, teaching Sunday school and summer Bible school and helping the sister workers conduct the regular Tuesday and Thursday evening Bible studies.

As is true in any congregation of any denomination, Diamond Street also had some difficulties. The cultural imperialism of a 1940s Lancaster Mennonite bishop caused many members, including Mattie's mother, considerable pain.[5] "In those early years, lots of adults came through Diamond Street, became members even," Mattie recounts. "But they just didn't last. It was such a great effort. The distinctive dress, you couldn't have insurance, you couldn't have another husband or wife somewhere else. You know, it was very difficult for adults whose lives had already been mixed up. It's not like they didn't come. They did come because Alma and Emma were staunch Bible teachers. They went out into homes all the time, and where the word of God was taught, people believed."

People did believe. They tuned in to the messages of hope emanating from the "Come to Jesus" church, which is what the neighborhood started calling the mission after a neon sign above the front door began flashing those words into the busy, shop-lined street.[6] Many believers such as Easter Jackson, who went back to the Methodist Church, moved on but never stopped speaking well of Alma and Emma and the work at Diamond Street. Encouraged by their mother, Mattie and her brothers stayed in the Mennonite church.

By fall 1961 many changes had come to Diamond Street. The federal government's notion that high-rise housing would solve the problems of city life led to the construction of several huge projects in north-central Philadelphia. Blight followed. Alma Ruth and Emma Rudy retired to a home for missionaries in Lancaster County. Luke and Miriam Stoltzfus solidified their connections to the neighborhood, taking over the vacant third-floor apartment as their family outgrew the second floor.

Mattie was in her mid-twenties. She had graduated from Jules Mastbaum Vocational Technical High School with a license to practice nursing. Working full time as an LPN, she poured most of her volunteer energies into the church. She taught Sunday school. She helped organize summer Bible school, working as superintendent several years. She chaired the church council. She was the librarian. One year the record book even noted that Mattie was church auditor.[7]

"Oh my, I forgot most of those things," says Mattie. "But yes, I do: I think of myself as a person with leadership gifts. I see myself using them automatically. For us, it's always been a matter of survival. Our women always had to take leadership. I mean, you take leadership or else you just die." For the Diamond Street Mennonite Church, which grew steadily during the mid-1960s, Mattie Cooper was a pillar of faith. She was a giving person, willing to put herself out for the children and young people of her neighborhood.

Like neighborhoods everywhere, the one around Diamond Street was alternately bathed in hope and despair, stability and transience. Most of the people who lived between Kensington and Fairmount Park were ordinary citizens committed to interracial cooperation and community-based improvement projects.[8] These deliberate and ongoing efforts to keep the neighborhood safe existed side-by-side with the disappointing reality that small business owners were leaving for suburban malls. They boarded up their shops, leading to an unwelcome influx of drug dealers with their imprint of corruption and instability. Diamond Street Mennonite Church continued to draw parishioners from a wide array of economic and ethnic backgrounds. Within easy walking distance of Temple University, it attracted both professors and students.

As the 1960s faded from the scene, those like Mattie who had grown up at Diamond Street assumed ever more prominent leadership positions. Change came naturally. Homer Schrock, the pastor who followed Luke Stoltzfus, left in December 1970. Raymond Jackson and Charles Baynard, husband of one of the Allen sisters who were Mattie's close friends, comprised the first black leadership team at Diamond Street.

As they had been doing from the beginning and became more able to do after Luke was ordained bishop, church members questioned the wisdom of importing Lancaster Mennonite cultural practices to their community. "When we were young, we didn't mind so much," says Mattie. "I think we sort of thought we were members of the Girl Scouts or some group like that. We were always explaining about Mennonites, and we gave the answers that Alma and Emma taught us, the verses in the Bible that corroborated their beliefs. I know this made us very strong, but when I grew to believe that this was no longer truth, I stopped doing it."

Although Mattie and others at Diamond Street stopped dressing in distinctive ways, they never stopped being a community- and service-oriented church. They sometimes chafed under the general Mennonite assumption that their church was a "mission outreach." Charles Baynard and Raymond Jackson worked very hard to change that perception. In 1975 when a pastor of Amish background succeeded Raymond, the people at Diamond Street continued their efforts to let the wider Mennonite world know that their church had always been solidly rooted in its surroundings. Charles Baynard and his new co-pastor, Freeman Miller, supported the church's ongoing desire to establish its own identity.

As chair of the church council, Mattie wrote a letter to the Eastern Board requesting two things: that the mission board change Freeman Miller's status from half-time to full-time pastor, and that the mission board allow Diamond Street to become a self-sufficient congregation, including giving over the deed to 1814 West Diamond Street.[9] The letters between Diamond Street and Eastern Board were quite cordial, but the memories of face-to-face and telephone conversations reveal some conflict as each tried to understand the other.[10]

The congregation asked why Eastern Board wanted to enter into a seven-year process leading to self-sufficiency. Why not just release the deed to the church? Eastern Board, on the other hand, expressed its concern that the community might not have a strong enough financial base to sustain the church. Why was the church in such a hurry? In many ways, it was a classic struggle between parent and child, a child long since living on its own.[11]

As for Mattie, she had other concerns, including an exhilarating opportunity to fulfill a lifelong dream—a dream that one day she could visit Africa. During the 1978 Mennonite World Conference in Wichita, a musical group from Kenya spent a weekend with the people of Diamond Street. Mattie hosted a young woman who told her an unforgettable story.

As members of the group gathered in Nairobi waiting for their flight to the United States, word came that the young woman's mother had died in childbirth and was already buried. What should she do? Should she give up the trip and go back to her family? One of the other team members comforted her by saying her mother would want her to have the experience. "It made such an impact on me," Mattie recalls. "I asked her why did her mother die?"

The young woman explained that many Kenyan villagers had only limited access to prenatal care. "And so I thought, 'Well, I don't have money to change the situation. But I do have a skill that I could give. I could go,'" Mattie explains. "At that point, I decided to look for avenues to serve in Africa. That's how I ended up with Mennonite Central Committee (MCC) in Burkina Faso."

Mattie had become an RN, completing her higher education and training at Community College of Philadelphia. She
would soon be forty-two years old, and the time seemed right
for an adventure. "I had always wanted to visit Africa, but
somehow it never occurred to me that I could just pack up and
go as a tourist. So I went as an MCC service worker." Mattie
worked in a hospital in Djibo.

The adventure turned into romance when Mattie met Ed
Nikiema. "Ed's father left Burkina as a young man and went to
Ghana to become a policeman there. When I arrived in Burkina
Faso, Ed had been living there for several years. He came back
because he wanted to get to know his roots—his father's people," Mattie says. "At that time, Burkina just didn't have private
enterprises, so Ed joined the military and was stationed in
Djibo. We met at the little Protestant church—the only Protestant church in town."

Ed Nikiema and Mattie Cooper were married in the courtyard of a friend's home on June 12, 1982. Mattie's voice becomes discernibly lighter as she describes the scene. "The house
belonged to Dr. Elliott at the Djibo hospital. His wife was a
botanist, and she worked very hard to keep flowers growing and
blooming. We filled the courtyard with chairs and benches, and
people crammed on in there for the ceremony."

When the Nikiemas moved to Philadelphia a year after the
wedding, they were just in time to participate in the transition
from the old church at 1814 two blocks east to a reconstructed
building at 1632 West Diamond Street. Inspired by their leadership team and members of the local community, the congregation managed to save a magnificent structure on this site from
the tenacious north Philadelphia wrecking ball. A former Bell
Telephone building, the Philadelphia Masonic Lodge had
owned and used the place before abandoning the neighborhood
in the mid-1970s, leaving both the site and structure to slow de-

cay. The lodge agreed to turn over the deed for one dollar if the people at Diamond Street could accumulate the funds for renovation.

They did. They set out to rebuild the interior, integrating their programs with neighborhood needs and opening the second floor as a new space for Sunday morning worship. Alma and Emma's "Come to Jesus" mission had an ambitious new identity as the Diamond Street Mennonite Church and Diamond Street Community Center.

Mattie reconnected quickly. Soon back in her comfortable lay leadership roles, she taught Sunday school, served on the community center's board, and sang in the choir. She took a job with the Visiting Nurses Association of Philadelphia. Her husband, a warm, friendly man with an open manner, also connected with Diamond Street. "He works two jobs right now. He's a security guard at Rite Aid, and he works nights for United Parcel Service," says Mattie. "Maybe soon he can give up one of those." Both Ed and Mattie continue to serve in a variety of leadership positions at their much-loved church.

In her decidedly straightforward and speak-the-truth style, Mattie declares, "I've never wanted to preach. But, you know, I probably do that, too. Certainly, on a small basis in small groups and places like that. I grew up in this church where we never had a wealth of male leaders, and I've been willing to fill opportunities that come up. I haven't felt deprived." Instead, she has been a consistent advocate for reconciliation and understanding, reaching across the differences people create to separate themselves from each other.

Mattie Nikiema does not support any of the stereotypes about north-central Philadelphia. From the day she arrived as a twelve-year-old girl, she has believed in this neighborhood. She sees evidence of hope on almost every street corner—vendors selling fresh produce on vacant lots, church sidewalk bazaars raising money by selling barbecued chicken and ribs, a brand-new, red-brick row house tucked between two much older city houses, the Messiah College Philadelphia campus occupying a renovated row along Broad Street just south of Diamond Street.

The high-rise projects have been demolished, replaced by an entire recreated row house community which covers vast blocks in the area immediately adjoining the eastern edge of the 1632 property. The local elementary school has more than seven hundred children. Mattie believes these children need the church. She is certain the church needs them. They are children, she maintains, with the same dreams and needs that Mattie and her friends had when they crowded into the rooms of the Mennonite mission to hear Alma Ruth and Emma Rudy teach the Bible.

This conviction has kept Mattie Nikiema at Diamond Street for nearly fifty years. "I've often asked myself why I've stayed when so many others have moved on," she muses now. "I'm a person that forms ties and puts down roots. This is the church where I found Christ, where I received my basic Bible teaching. I have a great attachment to the area, and I think it's important for the Mennonite church to stay in this community."

Elizabeth G. Nissley

Why Not Ordain Both of Us?

Elizabeth Landis Nissley
Mount Joy, Pennsylvania

SHE LINED THEM UP ON THE inside front stairway of their family home—her younger brother and sister and, on occasion, a male cousin. Elizabeth Landis loved to play church. "Let's join in 'Jesus Loves Me,'" she might sing out to begin the meeting. Then it was, "Turn in your pretend Bibles to Matthew 5 for a sermon on the 'Blessed Are Ye's' or Matthew 18 and working out your differences 'between thee and him alone.'" Prayers were offered extemporaneously and might include a plea for a small parishioner to pay attention or sit still. The youngsters did their best. They looked up to this slightly older sister, this girl who adored real church almost as much as their child-friendly, stair-step adaptation.[1] Elizabeth— Libby, as she came to be called—was born June 30, 1943. She and the rest of the Landis children understood the central place of the church in their lives.

Mennonite families of the 1940s and 1950s flocked to their local meetinghouses for entertainment, social interaction, and worship. Preachers consistently counseled members to avoid worldly amusements—fairs, festivals, movies, public school-sponsored dances, and athletic events. The church was a place to visit with family members and friends, to catch up on neighborhood affairs. It was also a center of hope, a vital connection to God, an island of refuge, a safe place. Young and old filled the pews for Wednesday night prayer meetings, Sunday morning services, and Sunday evening young people's meetings.

"My father's home congregation was Landis Valley, so that's where my parents put down roots," explains Libby. "Then during the gas rationing days of World War II, they could only drive all the way over there about once a month. Because our farm was much closer to East Petersburg, they tied into the Mennonite church in that town. By the time I was born, they were in the habit of participating in both churches. We went to Bible school at both places. Mom went to sewing circle at both places. We went to revival meetings at both places."[2]

Given Elam and Ruth Landis's love for the church, it was no wonder that the Landis children played church. Neither was it surprising that some of their seven children, including their third daughter Libby, developed aspirations for church work.

Her gifts for leadership and organization, vividly illustrated in her childhood playacting, posed many problems for this impressionable young woman. In early adolescence, she began to realize the high stakes of faithfulness. "I decided I didn't want to become a Christian because I'd have to join the church and change my appearance. I did not want that. But I also felt lots of guilt whenever I attended revival meetings. Then it happened when I was in seventh grade. I mean I stood for the invitation, and the next day I went to the local public school with a covering. That was one of the hardest days of my life. I hated, hated with a passion, putting my hair up."

That's what happened when Lancaster Mennonite girls accepted Christ in the mid-1950s. Congregations expected young women, who made new commitments, to immediately embrace Mennonite distinctives, shouldering the heavy burden of suddenly appearing in school with plain clothing. Some girls took it well. Some never joined the church. Some, like Elizabeth Landis, loved the church enough to struggle through the confusing midcentury as debates over the conference's *Rules and Discipline* and plain clothing became ever more heated.

Plainness of appearance and simplicity of life were not new concepts to the Lancaster Mennonite community. Frequent appeals, by way of the church paper, for members to dress plainly predated even the original 1881 *Rules and Discipline*. Before 1937, however, the document itself refrained from prescribing specific dress styles. Church members felt more free to ignore the pleas or to come up with their own versions of plain dress. In 1937 the Conference decided to spell out the requirements for plain dress, circulating a paper entitled "Standards of Dress of the Lancaster Conference of the Mennonite Church." In 1943 the paper's distinct requirements became part of the actual *Rules and Discipline* document.[3]

Although the instructions for men were somewhat open-ended, their dress rules were listed first. "That the Brethren wear the regulation coat, a plain hat. Avoiding anything that is worn for display, such as long neckties as well as flashy ties of any kind (we suggest omitting the tie). And seek to comply with that which they profess and in this way give a testimony against the vanity of the world."

Women were subjected to much more literal decrees. "The Sisters are to wear plain dresses made of material suitable for a plain dress. Capes are not to be omitted, skirts to be long and full enough to cover the form. Bonnets to be plain. Coverings should correspond to a plain bonnet. Round coverings are not allowed. Omitting ties on bonnets and coverings is a departure from this standard. Stylish hair dressing and wearing of jewelry is unscriptural. Stylish coats, shoes, and stockings are unbecoming to modesty and meekness of Spirit."[4]

So it was that a heightened rigidity around the questions of plain living became inseparably intertwined with church life. After 1937 congregational leaders walked on much different ground. Rather than making broad statements about humility and simplicity which allowed for wide fields of interpretation, leaders were required to read and recommend the specific written guidelines for the standards of dress. As the expectations grew and acceptable styles became more uniform, young girls such as Elizabeth Landis faced difficult personal questions. They wanted to respond to conviction. They needed peace, but they also sensed that something was not quite right.

The boys who stood with Libby and her cousin during those 1955 East Petersburg revival meetings awoke the next morning to completely different circumstances than the girls did. None of the boys' mothers arrived with hairpins and coverings to radically change their appearance. Although these young men were certainly expected to carry a witness to their schools, they were not required to wear the witness as a visible sign. Many Lancaster Mennonites—mothers, fathers, leaders, young people, and children—wondered about the wisdom of subjecting only the girls to such extreme changes.

These changes, championed throughout the first half of the twentieth century, were destined to be short-lived. It soon became apparent that the Lancaster Mennonite community was not prepared to completely disembark the train of modernity in the old-fashioned way of their Amish neighbors.

Although they dressed plainly, Lancaster Mennonites remained in step with the world in many other ways. They financed and promoted missions and mission workers. They liked being educated. They knew their way around the Lancaster business community, owning some of the most successful enterprises and farms in the county. They enjoyed technology—from tractors and cars to radios and even televisions. As their children—Libby and her peers—passed through adolescence, the tensions between who they were and how they looked slowly eroded the Lancaster Conference's carefully constructed plain fences.

"My family remembers everyone being ready to go to church. Libby and Mom would still be upstairs. I would be tearing at my covering or pulling out hairpins, demanding that she find a way to make it feel right. My mother went through something with me. I was always pushing the edges."

With her mother, Libby never hesitated to be clear and direct in communicating her desires. "I don't know for sure where that comes from," Libby reflects. "There were seven children, and I remember mealtime being fairly chaotic. I mean we didn't pass things in a convenient and orderly way. It was like, 'Hey, I need the potatoes down here!' You had to speak up for what you needed. But, you know, even within families there are differences. I've asked my siblings what they think about my place in the family. One thing is clear. I was the only one who had four years on either side of me. My mother had four years to anticipate me and four years to enjoy me. Maybe that's why I always could be direct with her."

The Landis family, while open and outspoken, came down on the conservative side of many church issues. Pushing the edges did not bring rewards. Libby learned to live with the dress requirements of the Landis Valley Mennonite Church. "I didn't understand. But I loved the church, so I complied."

In the fall of 1958, Libby enrolled at Lancaster Mennonite School as a high school sophomore. There, along with her peers, she discovered the wonders of exploration and inquiry while safely ensconced in the school's strict standards of dress and code of conduct.

As the social action and reaction of the 1960s crept into Lancaster congregations, the school and its supporters refused to budge. Its board and staff made few concessions to the sweeping changes that were beginning to swing Lancaster congregations back into mainstream society. The Sunday morning hair-pinning conflicts remembered by Libby's brothers and sisters grieved many other Mennonite parents in those days. Their children asked probing questions about the wisdom of wearing plain clothing in a fast-paced and troubled world. A tension not quickly resolved, the debates in these homes set the stage for a long-running drama.

For Libby high school was a happy time; a time of growing up and taking further steps to a life beyond Landis Valley and her family's East Petersburg farm. Though cloistered by a tightly bound church school, knowledge and learning cleared some of the haze from Libby's horizon, opening the first doors and windows to the world. When the 1961 seniors elected her class secretary, Libby's leadership and organizational skills blossomed and developed. She also met Ken Nissley.

From their days as high school sweethearts, Libby and Ken have been joined in a solid and ever more stable partnership. After graduation, Ken went off to Eastern Mennonite College (EMC) while Libby entered nurses' training at Lancaster General Hospital. Being so far apart was difficult, so they decided to get married. On August 13, 1964, friends and family members joined them on the lawn of the Ruth and Elam Landis family farm. "Getting married at home, rather than in a proper church wedding, was one indication of the alternative influences we felt as young Mennonites dealing with the 1960s," recalls Libby. "At home we could have flowers! I thought we had a beautiful wedding."

Libby and Ken went back to EMC together and began processing Ken's call to overseas missions. "That was definitely Ken's call rather than mine," Libby explains now. "But I knew without a doubt I wanted to go, to be with him."

Ken Nissley has often helped Libby make sense of their path from young lovers to 1960s idealists to mission workers in Somalia. He picks up the story: "Going to Somalia, getting out of the box, changed everything for us. We began to see the world as our community, not just Landis Valley or Mount Joy or Lancaster County Mennonites. For example, working in missions taught me to think about how women understand the church outside my childhood context."

Libby chimes in, "I think we were forever ruined by those experiences."

Forever ruined? What Libby means is the Mennonite farm community to which they returned in 1969, still grappling with plain clothing, did not hold much promise for them. She recalls their decision to live in Philadelphia. "We both decided to go back to school. I remember so clearly talking about it. I mean, we didn't have any money! But we did it."

During their time at the University of Pennsylvania, they also adopted Mark, their oldest child. Although they came home to Lancaster County often, a quick and easy way back into the Lancaster Mennonite box never appealed to either of them.

They lived in a changing north Philadelphia neighborhood. They learned their first lessons in parenting. They also finished degrees—Libby, a bachelor's in nursing; Ken, a master's in math education. "Throughout our time in the city, we both entertained the idea of returning to Somalia. Ken still felt called to mission work. So in 1970 we packed up Mark and left for Mogadishu, once again serving under Eastern Board. That term had some dreadful lows, mostly because I had a hard time finding my place at the mission," says Libby with some pain. "It almost tore Ken and me apart."

The term also had some stimulating highs. A major charismatic revival swept the Somali mission. In this climate, Libby and Ken tuned in to a fresh work of the Spirit. They renewed their marriage, strengthening the unique cord of spirituality that encapsulates Libby Nissley's perception of personal faith.

"We were in a real spiritual vacuum at the time of the Somali revival. We really needed the charismatic experience. So it feels like I've tasted many streams. Where am I now? I'm not sure if I have a name to describe it. I'm not in the charismatic stream, but I'm also not completely in the practical stream. Maybe I'll just call it a very active ministry stream."

As an active minister of God's grace, Libby practices a pragmatic Christian faith, worshiping a benevolent God—a God who inspires her to treat others with compassion and respect, who understands when she doesn't spend twenty minutes a day praying, and who expects conservation of the earth's resources. She also relies on a supernatural faith, worshiping a mysterious God—a God who bathes her soul and spirit with love, who responds when she finds time for long, silent prayer retreats, who cannot be described but must be experienced.

This union between active social responsibility and utter dependence on the God of spiritual renewal sustains Libby Nissley. It holds her life together. It's one of the reasons she and Ken built on their spiritual experience in Somalia by choosing to live in an intentional community.

"We knew Herb and Sarah Myers from college. They were very interested in all that 1970s alternative lifestyle stuff. They wrote to us while we were in Somalia. When we were ready to come home, Ken took a job at Salunga [Eastern Board's home office]. We talked to Herb and Sarah and agreed to try communal housing. Together, we bought this house [the Mount Joy home where the Nissleys still live] where we shared a kitchen and community space from 1975-1978."

Libby says their choice to live in an intentional community made them suspect among Lancaster Mennonites. "I remember my dad coming here one evening and accusing me of being a hippie. But, you know, the thing about my dad—as soon as he got home, he called and apologized. This whole thing of two families living together; it just didn't make sense to him. And the truth is, we were idealistic and too critical of others sometimes. We were trying to make a transition from another culture back into Lancaster County life."

Again, Ken helps Libby clarify their story, "We were idealistic, that's true. But we were also seriously committed as Christians. We still believe that conservation and simple living make a lot of sense. We think it's important to work and worship where we have our home."

The witness of their words is best understood in Libby and Ken's lifelong commitment to simple living and in their equal commitment to mission work. Ken stayed at the home office in Salunga for ten years. During this time, they adopted two more children, Andy and Becca. When Becca was ready for kindergarten, Libby thought she might go back to school—until she discovered she was pregnant.

"This is hard for me to say, but I was so angry. I mean all those years and never pregnant. Then just when I'm ready to move on with my life, I'm pregnant." Her voice is tinged with the sharp disappointment of receiving a much- longed-for gift at what seems to be an inconvenient time.

Two things helped bring perspective to Libby's dilemma. "One of my dear friends gave me a notebook and said, 'Start journaling. All your life you've tried to be in touch with what's going on inside you. Don't stop now.'" Then four months into the pregnancy, she fell down a couple of steps. The shock of realizing she could lose the child sharpened her focus. Her frustrations dissolved in thankfulness, and her anger dissipated as quickly as it had come.

"Our children are such an important part of my life. I would not want to be without a single one of them," she says now. "Ken and I thought we would adopt and provide a nice, loving environment that would take care of the ills of the world for these children. Well, it hasn't always worked that way. Maybe we're better people for it. We understand grief and pain much more easily, I think."

Libby's voice changes as she describes mothering her children; it becomes much stronger. An almost imperceptible shift in the expression on her face precedes an urgent lesson in resourceful parenting. "We do not own our children. Our images are not dependent on how they live. What matters is that we love them, that we have a relationship with them. This is what I tell people who come to me for advice." Every story that Libby Nissley tells about her four grown children opens a door to yet another dimension in the rich rooms of light and love these young people have brought to this missionary wife become nurse become mother and pastor.

When Sara, their youngest daughter, turned four, Ken and Libby began pining for East Africa again. On their first two assignments to Somalia, the Nissleys joined a large, well-established Mennonite mission. Each time Eastern Board had invited Ken to teach in the mission school, making the breakthrough decision not to ordain him as they had previously done with every man who signed on for mission work.

Libby tagged along as his wife. "When we arrived at Jowhar the first time, we had been married two years. We thought we'd have children. It was assumed I would move into the traditional role of missionary wife. The mission board and the Somali people knew what to do with missionary men, even those who weren't ordained. They knew what to do with single women. They didn't know what to do with wives who didn't have children. It was not easy for me."

By the time Libby and Ken agreed to a third term in 1983, the political climate in Somalia had changed. The large Mennonite mission was gone, summarily dissolved when the government nationalized all hospitals and schools in the early 1970s. Ken and Libby's personal expectations had also changed. So had their family life. They had four children, so it seemed obvious to the Eastern Board that Libby would be a busy missionary mother and wife.

Explaining the shift in their personal calling to Eastern Board proved a formidable task. During their prior assignments, Libby had been following what was more specifically Ken's call. When they started talking about going back in the early 1980s, the Nissleys soon sensed an equal calling to return to this nomadic, sub-Saharan country with its miles and miles of Indian Ocean shoreline. "The decision to go back to Somalia in 1983 was so different for us. Ken and I believed we were being called to a partnership in mission. That's when we asked the question."

The question would ignite all the long-dormant yearnings for pastoral work in Libby Nissley's heart. Together, they approached Eastern Board. After affirming Ken's and Libby's desire to return, the mission board immediately inquired whether Ken should be ordained. The Nissleys asked, "But we hear this call jointly, so why not ordain both of us?"

Ordaining a woman was unheard-of in the Lancaster Conference. The shock waves must have been deep, but Ken was a respected staff person at Eastern Board's home office, and their query was not easily dismissed. Instead, it generated lots of discussion. "I mean, we were clearly naive when we asked that question," says Libby. "Even though we both grew up in Lancaster County, our perspective just wasn't grounded in reality."

In one meeting a principal Eastern Board person even said, "Well, I don't think it'll be a problem." Ken immediately sensed that something had not connected. He asked, "Wait a minute—what are you talking about?" Though the conversation had centered on both Libby and Ken being ordained, the person replied, "Well, we'll ordain you and commission Libby."

Libby sighs long and slowly as she continues the story. "You know, it was just as if none of the dialogue about ordination had even taken place. We were disappointed, but we decided to submit. Ken was ordained, and I was commissioned. We left for Somalia with our family. For the next three years, we worked as partners as we believed God called us."

They each worked in Somali government institutions. In mutually supportive roles, they carried the burden and call of both their home and the small believers group. They hosted Somali friends, served on the church council, prepared lots of tea and fellowship meals, and took turns preaching and teaching. "The fact that Ken was ordained and I was not made very little difference in the day-to-day needs and work of our Somali church."

The same was not true when they returned to southeastern Pennsylvania for the third time in 1986. Libby and Ken Nissley were coming to a more settled place in their personal journeys. Some of their 1960s idealism had dissipated, and their commitment to the church had grown. They came home once again to the region of their birth, to the Mount Joy Mennonite Church, and to the Lancaster Mennonite Conference.

The Nissleys inquired about jobs in the Lancaster area. "Ken got several invitations to pastor churches, but he was clear. He didn't want to be involved in church ministry. I did feel called, but of course no invitations came to me."

To separate themselves from this confusing disparity, Ken accepted a computer programming position at an office supply store. Libby took a nursing position at Philhaven Hospital in Mt. Gretna, Pennsylvania. She also commuted from Mount Joy to the University of Pennsylvania, where she completed a master's degree in psychiatric mental health nursing in 1989.

"I did think about leaving the conference to see if I could find work in some other church or denomination. I still think about that sometimes," Libby muses. "But you know, this is where I grew up. This is where my history and my home are. I understand these people. I love this conference. Leaving would be excruciating for both Ken and me."

This devotion to her people is one of the most fascinating themes in Libby Nissley's personal narrative. She longs to share her gift for congregational leadership with her own people, the people of the Lancaster Mennonite Conference. After living quietly with this desire for most of her life, a wonderful thing happened in October 1993. The congregation Libby and Ken chose as adults—Mount Joy Mennonite—invited her to be their minister of pastoral care. Both excited and terrified, Libby took the risk and accepted the half-time assignment.

Her work at Mount Joy centers around counsel and nurture. She has a pastor's soul; she can preach; she can rally people around a cause. She is caring and loving and, above all else, discreet. Although Libby often speaks openly about her work, she never discloses details that would identify the people she serves. Ever clear and direct, she is quick to say, "I cannot talk about that."

When she preaches, her sermons carry the imprimatur of a woman convinced of God's unconditional love, of humankind's response to this love. In a message titled "How Then Should We Love?" delivered on Sunday morning, September 15, 1996, she said, "This unconditional love is a love of extravagance. I want Mount Joy Mennonite Church to be a place where anyone, all kinds of people are welcome. Not because we are so good or wonderful or even welcoming, but because we have experienced and accepted Jesus' love and then are willing to pass it on whenever and wherever possible to others. So that people in this community can say, 'Look how those followers of

Jesus at Mount Joy Mennonite love—I want to go and be with them and learn about the One who is changing them.'"[5] Spoken like a woman who has taken water from many streams and who knows the value of active ministry.

Much of Libby's pastoral energy focuses on the organizational parts of church leadership, bringing committees and groups together and blessing them in their work. "I get lots of excitement out of being a helper to others. I like organizing tasks in concert with others. I love telling people, 'You did a good job,' and asking, 'How can we do it better?'"

Keenly aware that the Lancaster Conference has not been ready to recognize her call as deserving ordination and open public endorsement, Libby and Ken continue to struggle with the fact that people in their community oppose the reality of women in leadership. They hope for change so their daughters and sons will not be saddled with this particular piece of Lancaster Mennonite culture.

Libby has little desire to be a trailblazer, repeatedly saying that she only wants the freedom to do her work and do it well. "I would wish for a little less background noise. It's always disconcerting when people express dissatisfaction with my gender. But criticism is part of leadership, and I am learning to be less reactive. My dear husband helps me so much with this."

Ken understands what she feels and what she means. "After I was ordained for the Somali work, when Libby wasn't, I started thinking much more consciously about which one of us had the gifts for congregational leadership. I am sure one of us is a pastor, and it's not me. It's Libby."

Miriam E. Book

12

My Spirit Soared

Miriam Book
Elkhart, Indiana

MIRIAM BOOK GREW UP IN the church. Her parents, Harold and Cora Book, lived and breathed worship, community, congregational dynamics, and even Mennonite Church politics. "They *loved* the church!"[1] Mim declares. "They never, ever, would have left." The youngest of six children, Mim was born April 27, 1948. Like many Lancaster Mennonite children, she was carried to worship services and church functions from the time she was a few weeks old.

Harold, a farmer-preacher, and Cora, his homemaker partner, complemented and supported each other's hospitality and leadership gifts. They gave their equal and faithful devotion to Lancaster County's Paradise Mennonite Church, where Harold was ordained and where he preached for more than twenty years. They raised their daughter Miriam to have the same devotion and respect for the church.

As a young person, she often sat at the dining room table or on the living room sofa as they entertained churchwide leaders such as J. C. Wenger, George R. Brunk II, and Paul N. Kraybill. She admired both of her parents for their openness and warmth, their gracious way of receiving visitors and making people feel at home. She listened as her father suggested unconventional solutions to the multidimensional problems of church and community life. Learning from his courage, Mim acquired an unswerving loyalty to the church.

Harold Book also taught his daughter that loyalty was not useful if it was blind. Allegiance to the church, he showed by example, must always be tempered by the desires and needs of ordinary people. "The church was not perfect for Mom and Dad," recalls Mim. "Both the good and bad were included in our dinner table conversations. If Dad didn't talk after a district meeting, I knew he had probably taken a lone position on a difficult issue. He tried not to get hung up on small questions. He always had a larger vision."

Although Harold respected church structure and its channels of communication, he also considered the sincerity of conviction in individual believers. In his work at Paradise, he met people with many needs and questions—needs and questions for which he and other church leaders seldom had simple answers. Sometimes after discussing an unusual request with his fellow ministers or the conference bishops, Harold would go ahead and follow his leadership instincts—like the time he agreed to baptize a new believer in the Book farm pond.

The woman he baptized, a lawyer from New York, came to personal faith through the efforts of a Paradise-area Mennonite family who hosted tourists in their home. She explained to Harold that the Lancaster Mennonite tradition of baptizing by pouring seemed inadequate to her, and she requested immersion.

"Dad always said, 'If a person's heart is sincere, why not?'" Mim vividly remembers the day of the baptism—the green meadow, the blue sky, the mud on the bank of the pond. "It was a sunny Sunday afternoon, but it had rained that week. I remember it was hard for Dad and Goldie to go down the slippery side of the pond. About fifteen or twenty of us sat on the nearby grass, taking it all in. I suppose I was in my early twenties. I will never forget my dad's respect for Goldie Rotenberg and her very personal request."

Cora and Harold Book owned and operated a family farm a few miles north of Strasburg, near the geographic and historical center of the Lancaster Mennonite community. On their farm, everyone—parents, Mim, her four older sisters, and one older brother—tackled the work, generating few discussions about whether or not a specific job was men's or women's work. When a heifer needed help calving, when the alfalfa was ready, when the cornfields turned dry in early fall, everyone—women and men—pitched in. An atmosphere of shared responsibility and equality of experience enveloped the house and farm.

"There on the farm I gained many of the skills I use today," Mim says. "We always worked in teams. Not that we called it working in teams! But in the fields, baling hay, or whatever—helping a cow give birth, nurturing her, and making sure that small calf and mother were okay. Those were things we did together." Management happened in partnership, falling on the wide shoulders of both father and mother.

The Lancaster Mennonite community nurtured dozens of women like Mim Book—women raised on vibrant family farms where their gifts were needed and used. These women generally came to believe gender roles would move, as they do on the farm, in response to need. "There was never any question that I could do the farm work. I was needed. It's the same in the church. I don't care whether we're women or men, the church needs our gifts."

The church needs people of both genders to exercise their gifts whatever they may be: that's what Mim believes. That's what she internalized from her days of driving tractors, planting gardens, and tilling fields. That's what she saw in action when the Book family spent its summer holidays serving an outpost vacation Bible school in northern Pennsylvania.

"The Paradise church would put up this large tent and invite the local community to a Mennonite summer Bible school," recalls Mim. "As far back as I can remember, I was pulled into leadership in that setting; whether it was teaching children's classes, telling flannelgraph stories, or helping Mom with her classes. I never once thought about gender differences."

It's hard to imagine now, but Mim was a shy, rather solitary child and young person. Four years younger than her next older sister, she struggled mightily with the typical teenage blues. "My self-esteem was not whole," she explains now. She sometimes thought herself inferior to the other young people who surrounded her at Lancaster Mennonite School.

During her last year at LMS, Mim attended a weeklong servanthood work camp in Washington, D.C., a summer voluntary service assignment sponsored by Eastern Board. "One night I lied," she admits with eyes twinkling and mouth moving into an embarrassed grin, "and asked the group to pray for a friend of mine who didn't know whether or not she was a Christian. Here were these people, who I had just learned to know, praying earnestly for Mim's friend, who was really me. It's amazing and unbelievable, but how I saw the world changed from that moment on. Healing my self-esteem has been a continuing process, but that evening in Washington something converted inside me. I knew it was salvation. When I came home, I did better in school. I got my act together. I felt better about myself."

She also wrestled with a consistent and well-defined call from God. The call first came during one of the annual family treks to northern Pennsylvania. "We had several of our meetings in a church that summer. I remember the stained glass windows and the cross at the front. I remember singing that song, 'I have decided to follow Jesus. No turning back, no turning back.' I couldn't have been more than six years old, but it was a holy moment, my first awareness of God. Something special happened to me in that little country church."

As she tells of her call to leadership, Miriam Book's voice speeds up, and she talks in a rapid flow of words, punctuated by phrases that underline the significance of her experience. "Paradise was one of the prime places that helped to launch the mission movement, and I have memories of missionaries coming back to the States and telling their stories, giving their testimonies. They were often single women. So I never thought I couldn't be a leader in the church. It was obvious God called these women; it was an energy from inside. That just caught me—that passion."

Catching the passion set Mim on a sometimes exhilarating, sometimes exhausting personal journey. As a young adult, she signed up for an interdenominational seminar on women's growth and self-esteem. "During that weekend I felt God's call to what I then labeled women's ministries. I envisioned myself leading, encouraging, and pointing persons to Christ. I did not struggle with whether it was appropriate for me as a woman to lead."[2]

She had seen shared leadership modeled in her home. She had heard women like Phebe Yoder, Catharine Leatherman, and Miriam Wenger tell their fascinating stories of witnessing for Jesus in Africa. "I did struggle, however, with my own self-understanding, for I was shy and withdrawn and found myself saying, as Mary did to the angel in giving birth to the child Jesus, 'But how can this be?'"[3]

Then she told her parents about her call to leadership. "Dad had stepped away from the dinner table, and Mom called him back, 'Mim has something she wants to share with you.' Dad stood there and said, 'Well, well, well,' as he does when something moves him. Mom looked at me and said, 'Well, Miriam, maybe someday you can take Dad's place in the church.'"

From that moment, Miriam Book's parents acknowledged and defended their daughter through the many queries she faced. "I cannot talk about my call without also talking about my parents and their undivided support for me," she says.

Like many Mennonite congregations, the Paradise Mennonite Church had serious questions about women in leadership. Mim shared her sense of call with a few trusted friends and found responses ranging from restrained words of love to rather strong feelings that she should not pursue the idea.

At the time, she was confused and hurt. Later in life, she realized that many Lancaster Mennonite congregations—indeed, many congregations in the churchwide Mennonite community—struggled with similar opposing influences and opinions regarding the recognition of women's gifts. She concentrated her dreams and hopes on the opportunities and possibilities that were open to her.

"I read everything I could find on women in the church, women and self-esteem, women and our sense of identity." After working her way to the glass ceiling in a Lancaster-area printing company, she said yes to Eastern Board when they invited her to work in their home offices in Salunga, Pennsylvania. "At the time, I also had a deep knowing that it was okay to be single. People heard about it, and I received lots of invitations to speak about singleness. You know, that's a topic not many people are willing to talk about."

So it was that Mim launched a speaking career and public ministry with a subject that gave pause to many church leaders. The integrity and purpose with which she shared her story captured the attention of audiences and opened the doors to other kinds of ministry. "It was God's work in my life. It was not me, it was God through me. It was the power of the Holy Spirit."

As she began to feel more confident, Mim agreed to challenging new assignments and requests. She also met other women whose personal testimonies and words of love energized and inspired her. While serving on the Lancaster-area Women's Missionary and Service Commission (WMSC), for example, she learned to know Mary Lauver. "Mary came to me one time and told me she saw something special in my life, in my spiritual person. I know her affirmation helped fan the flame of my call."

After being elected president of the Lancaster Conference WMSC, Mim cooperated with several other women to form a group called Business and Professional Women, an important source of support for the hundreds of Lancaster Mennonite women who became business and professional people during the bustling 1970s and 1980s. Eventually, Mim was called to serve the Mennonite Church WMSC, based in Elkhart, Indiana. "I know that saying yes to each opportunity as it came paved the way to that later invitation to work for the denomination," she reflects now.

Mim's work with Eastern Board took her to numerous Mennonite congregations from North America to East Africa, from California to Ontario, from Tanzania to Ethiopia to Kenya. She led youth retreats. She spoke to both women and men about the work of missions. She influenced young and old to follow the call of God in their lives.

When Paul Zehr, a Lancaster Conference bishop, invited her to preach in a local congregation during a series on prayer, Mim took the risk and said yes. "Trusted church leaders are central to women's journeys, but we women must also say yes," she says with conviction. "That's the really hard part sometimes, but I wouldn't be where I am today if I had said no."

In the early 1980s, Mim decided to leave Eastern Board and go back to school. She obtained an undergraduate degree at Eastern College in St. Davids, Pennsylvania, and then worked as director of marketing at Philhaven Hospital, a health and mental wellness facility in Mt. Gretna, Pennsylvania. "Because one of my jobs was making connections to Lancaster Conference congregations, I accepted many invitations to speak on Sunday mornings," says Mim. "It was there, in those churches, that my spirit soared."

In 1989, with her spirit still soaring, Mim accepted the Mennonite Church General Board's invitation to become Associate General Secretary at the denominational headquarters in Elkhart, Indiana. She was among the first women working in the inner circle of the Mennonite Church, a denomination with great respect for the hierarchy of influence and leadership that flows from its central offices to the twenty-one regional conferences and 1,000-plus congregations.

As she travels and works in the North American Mennonite community, Mim carries with her the lessons about teamwork and tolerance she learned among rural Lancaster County Mennonite farmers. Her people and their wisdom enrich her worldview. Though it is not always easy, she believes that focusing on broader ideas and visions is much more important than choosing single issues for divisive and unbroken discussion. "I constantly remind myself that if I can have half the vision my dad had for the church, I will be an effective leader."

Regularly, she visits each of the Mennonite Church conferences. She preaches and teaches, sits on committees, and helps guide decisions that affect individual conferences and the entire denomination. Her determination and insight, combined with an ability to hear and respect other points of view, serve the church well in its efforts to stay current and relevant for the thousands of young people born into its homes and attracted to its doors each year.

In 1992, after three years with the General Board, she was asked whether she would consider ordination. "I just sort of melted. All those years I knew I was called by God. I loved the

church, and now my faith community recognized and understood."

Jim Lapp, Mim's supervisor at the time, asked her to share
the story of her call with the elders of her congregation, Belmont Mennonite Church. "It was the first time in years that I
thought about my call or my young adult experiences around
the question of women in leadership. As I began to talk, I broke
down in sobs. They had to go on to a different question because
I couldn't go on," Mim recalls. "The next day several people,
including Paul Gingrich, called and talked to me. I realized that
I had repressed a vital part of myself. And here were all these
people—Jim, Paul, my pastor Duane Beck, and others—saying,
'No, Mim, your call is valid. Valid!'" With each articulation of
the word *valid*, Mim's voice ascends further up the scale, pulsat-
ing with an energy born of conviction and perseverance.

On Sunday morning, August 16, 1992, she was ordained at
Belmont Mennonite Church. Her parents stood next to her,
laying their hands on this daughter they had raised to realize
and seize the fullness of life. Her colleagues from the General
Board, relatives from Lancaster County, and friends from Elkhart and beyond came to fill the pews at 1527 Belmont Avenue,
participating in the passion and privilege of a pivotal moment in
Miriam Book's story. Her church had legitimized her call.

A powerful combination of passion and privilege guides
Mim Book today. From her holy moment with God when she
was six years old, to her high school experience with assurance
of salvation, to her adult certainty of the call of God, she's come
a long way. It is not by accident that she holds one of the more
influential positions in the Mennonite Church.

"And yes, I do have influence, impact, and power," Mim
acknowledges with her customary and disarming directness. "If
I refuse to recognize this, I am not being a good steward of my
authority." Mim refuses to hide behind the more common Men-

nonite supposition that power identified may cause pride, maintaining that the "power causes pride" philosophy fails to comprehend an all-too-obvious truth—influence and power cannot be separated from each other. Power denied, she says, often quickly goes awry, hurting those in its path while it sometimes carries on unchecked for generations. That potential is what Mim means to acknowledge when she speaks so boldly about personal influence and power.

In June 1998, she applied for and was accepted in the Shalem Institute's two-year Soul of the Executive program. Designed to encourage personal renewal and build a long-term spiritual framework for organizational leaders, the program offers a combination of residential and at-home learning. Much of the program happens at home in a guided study tailored to meet each person's needs and professional background. Mim plans to schedule parts of a sabbatical to coincide with the Institute's residential and retreat experiences.

Meanwhile, changes in Mennonite Church structure, including integration with a large sister denomination—the General Conference Mennonite Church—promise to redefine Mim's career. Her eyes and gestures reflect the warm hope of one who believes the best is yet to come. "I expect a whole new level of career decisions to open for me," she says with confidence.

No longer awkward and shy, Miriam Book is a woman who believes in herself, a woman whose opinions and stories reveal a complex kaleidoscope of colors and images—an ordinary Lancaster County farm girl, a person with influence, a one-of-a-kind, original Mennonite church leader.

Janet M. Breneman

13

Training Leaders in Central America

Janet Breneman
Guatemala City, Guatemala

"From as far back as I can remember in my childhood, I somehow had a sense of call to overseas ministry," Janet Breneman reflects. "I'm sure I was influenced by hearing missionary stories in our church at Masonville. Bertha Beachy [longtime Eastern Mennonite Missions worker] was one of my mentors. As a child, I remember praying for her and the work she was doing in Somalia."[1]

Neither has Janet Breneman forgotten the day she told one of her mother's friends that she wanted to be a missionary when she grew up. "My parents were quite surprised, I think. To be invited to do mission work was considered an honor. It wasn't a vocation people talked about openly. It just wasn't appropriate to announce that you wanted to be a missionary, even if you were only nine or ten."

The midcentury Lancaster mission culture, so carefully cultivated by Henry Garber and those before him, was one in which young women and men were approached with invitations. People seldom applied or volunteered; they were asked to go. Eastern Board leaders looked for faithfulness of life, an interest in Bible study, and sincere expressions of Christian conviction. Being called to the mission field was not something to take lightly. Janet's parents changed the subject, encouraging her to wait until some later time to think about mission work.

Although Jean and Clifford Breneman wondered briefly at their daughter's unusual aspirations, they had other more pressing concerns. Born June 6, 1949, Janet was the oldest of five children. Clifford worked as a mason, and he and Jean settled close to the Breneman homestead in Lancaster County's Manor Township, teaching their children to appreciate both the church and their surrounding community.

Awash in the flow of rural culture, many of the Breneman family's friends and neighbors retained the memories of land deeded to them by William Penn.[2] More than two hundred years had passed, but it was not unusual for Mennonites who lived in Penn's Conestoga Manor to have stayed on or close to nine- and ten-generation family farms. The Manor played host to a stable agrarian community, a place where neighbors depended on neighbors and where church, land, and family were embraced.

Janet and her siblings participated in an active youth group called the Manor Christian Workers Band. Each year they tilled popcorn, squash, sweet corn, and tomatoes on a plot of donated land which they, in the language of 1950s and 1960s Mennonite youth groups, called "the Lord's acre." They operated food stands at farm sales and washed and waxed cars to raise money. Gifts were sent to Eastern Board's voluntary service program, the Mennonite Home, the Millersville Children's Home, and directly to mission workers such as Mahlon and Mabel Hess in Tanganyika.[3]

Completely enmeshed in church and family, Janet and her Manor-area friends fit the mold of most midcentury Lancaster Mennonite young people. They went to church. They dressed in distinctive plain fashions. They enjoyed each other's company. Located on the far western edge of the community, the Masonville congregation was also far enough from the geographic center of the Lancaster Conference to foster some freedom of expression, creating an interesting dichotomy—groups to both the left and right of the mainstream Lancaster Mennonite way.

The Manor District bishop who baptized Janet, Benjamin C. Eshbach, helped to found the ultraconservative Mennonite Messianic Mission, precipitating the 1968 withdrawal of a large group from the Lancaster Conference, including folks from Masonville. Their goals included establishing a more plain and pure body of believers. Now called the Eastern Pennsylvania Mennonite Church, this movement sought to preserve the conservative dress and life standards championed by the Great Awakening revival preachers.

In vivid contrast, Janet's experience of the Masonville community prepared her for a relatively progressive view of what it meant to be Mennonite. "I see Masonville as having been surprisingly open to women, for example. I had good women role models as Sunday school teachers. Mahlon Hess is from my church, and he was always very encouraging of my leadership gifts," she recalls.

Janet doesn't have a distinct memory of a specific call from God, but she always tried to be present when Eastern Board and other mission workers came and talked to students at Lancaster Mennonite School and Eastern Mennonite College. "After the meetings, I would seek out the missionaries or the mission board representatives and ask them specific questions: What should I study if I wanted to go overseas? What would be most useful?"

During her sophomore year of college, Janet heard about an option to study abroad for a year. She decided to spend her junior year at Haile Selassie I University in Addis Ababa, Ethiopia. "That, I think, was a bit out of the ordinary for Lancaster Mennonites, but I made the decision with the idea that I would probably go overseas someday," Janet recalls. "I remember calling my parents to tell them I would really love to go."

Jean and Clifford Breneman immediately offered their support. "Well, we expected you would go overseas sometime. We're not surprised by this." The grass, they knew, seldom grew under their twenty-year-old daughter's feet. She was not one to wait around or waste time. Janet moved forward with her plans, her eyes firmly fixed on making the most of a rich opportunity to live in another part of the world.

The year in Ethiopia heightened her awareness on many levels. She wrote home of university courses called "Societies in Africa" and "African Literature," of casual conversations with mission leaders who also stayed at the Mennonite Guest House as they passed through Addis, and of a vacation with Peg Groff at Sodere, a hot springs resort where the two women spent an evening "watching the monkeys jump from tree to tree."[4]

The courses taught from an African point of view inspired Janet to approach the absolutes of her American Mennonite education with important cultural questions. The interactions with leaders of various Mennonite missions laid the foundation for Eastern Board's later confidence in her abilities and gifts. The friendships with women like Arlene Kreider and Peg Groff grew into lifelong relationships of mutuality and trust. Enlightened and revived, Janet came home to finish her coursework at EMC. She set her heart on one day returning to Ethiopia.

"When I graduated from college, I had Ethiopia in the back of my mind. But how, I asked myself, was this going to happen? How do I make this happen? If I make this happen, is that really God calling?" Meanwhile, her Lancaster County home community beckoned. LMS invited Janet to join its faculty as a home economics instructor. She agreed and moved back into her parents' house, commuting the thirty-some miles round-trip to her first professional job.

It was a fascinating and turbulent time to be a young Mennonite woman in Lancaster County. After the 1968 division, the main Mennonite body, including the folks who stayed at Masonville, rather quickly moderated dress and lifestyle requirements. The long-disputed *Rules and Discipline* disappeared from church discourse and polity. By the early 1970s, many Lancaster Mennonite young people dressed according to current fashions and trends. They abandoned most of the traditional taboos, including those against going to fairs, sports events, and theaters.

Some were deeply affected by the anti-Vietnam War efforts, participating in marches and rallies and asking church leaders questions most had never dreamed would come up in their congregations. The high school, as had been its custom, remained a citadel to conservatism, forbidding interscholastic sports and organized drama and requiring the young people to conform to dress codes no longer practiced in their home churches. In spite of the school's conservatism, the rapid and vast changes in the neighboring Mennonite community extended an aura of freedom tempered by recurring questions about what women could and could not do.

The young women at Masonville, for example, began cutting and styling their hair very soon after the 1968 division.[5] But to teach at the high school in 1972 and 1973, Janet was required to have long hair and wear a covering. "I changed more slowly than some," she recalls. "I think I've always been too conscientious to change without carefully weighing all the possibilities. Too careful, maybe!" She did not cut her hair until some years later.

Before Janet could become too involved in Lancaster County's contentious climate of change, she received her long-awaited invitation to overseas mission work. "It wasn't quite what I expected. I had always imagined I would go back to Ethiopia. Then Beth Eby, an EMC classmate and close friend, asked me to go to Honduras and take over the Eastern Board Voluntary Service (VS) position she had filled in the village of Tocoa. We had both completed home economics majors at EMC, and she thought I would like working with women's groups in health and nutrition development. I said yes." Going to Tocoa, Honduras, in 1973 was a life-changing experience for Janet. She gave herself to the work, presenting health and nutrition classes to school and women's groups.

About a year after Janet arrived, Hurricane Fifi upset the mission's programs when it made direct landfall on the eastern Honduran coastline. A small town about twenty miles inland, Tocoa and the surrounding area absorbed the full brunt of the 1974 storm. Janet and Judith Sarmiento, her Honduran colleague, had traveled from Tocoa to Rio Esteban, a tiny, ocean-side village, to give one of their women's health courses. "There were news reports and warnings. But we had not heard them."

The women were caught between two rising rivers and the ocean as the hurricane's fierce rain and wind battered the coast. "I remember being incredibly scared. I couldn't believe how calm the people in the village were. They knew there was nothing to do except hunker down. So that's what we did."

After the storm passed, Janet and Judith still couldn't leave because of high water and rough seas. Janet's family became increasingly worried because the central VS unit in La Ceiba had not heard from them. No one knew where they were until they walked into the unit house four days after the hurricane.

Several thousand people died during Hurricane Fifi. The aftermath with its devastation was a difficult time for the missionaries, who were mostly involved in relief work for about a year and a half. It wasn't quite what Janet imagined she would do as an overseas mission worker, but it helped prepare the soil for what became her fervent conviction that missionaries should not be lifted up as people who were more saintly or more called of God than those whom they were sent to serve.

Grounded in the truths of her experiences, Janet hoped to work with, not above, the national leaders of Central American churches. "My work has been in development—with women's groups when I was in VS and later in leadership training. I do not see myself in a superior role. I've always wanted to work alongside the national brothers and sisters."

In May 1975, she said farewell to her friends in Tocoa and headed east for La Ceiba, where the Mennonites were opening a vocational institute. Numerous Mennonite mission outposts throughout Honduras had established small Bible institute training centers. As they expanded, workers began sharing a dream to improve the economic situation of the emerging leaders by using mission dollars to teach vocations as well as Bible. Why not purchase land and put up some buildings? Why not house Bible and vocational studies at the same central location? The leaders in the States dispatched several workers in the early 1970s to build classrooms and implement the vision.

The philosophies of the institute matched Janet's own belief system, and she gladly agreed to develop the home economics department. "I worked there three years, learning along with the first graduating class. We had five students who started and finished the program. During our second year, we instituted an orientation process where the girls and boys had to rotate for six weeks through each of the different departments. Some of the girls actually decided to study carpentry and agronomy. But none of the boys ever chose home ec! That would have been a stretch in their *machista* culture."

After visiting the Mennonite Vocational Institute in early 1977, Grace Kauffman described Janet's classroom for the readers of Eastern Board's *Missionary Messenger*: "Amid mac-ramé planters, handcrafted blouses, skirts, purses, and painted seeds was the Home Economics Department—the cheeriest of all classrooms, clearly having the touch of a woman's hand." In her curriculum, Janet tried to balance abstract learning and re-ality, striving to teach the young women skills that would im-prove their communities and lives. To Grace she offered a pre-view of the theology she was beginning to own. "The girls need to learn it's beautiful to be a woman. Women weren't meant to be trampled on by men, as this culture often believes."[6]

Observing the oppression of women through a Latin American lens, Janet also learned of similar struggles among some of her sisters in the Lancaster Mennonite community. She began to re-imagine her personal call, navigating the path to change as carefully as she traversed the mountainous Honduran roads. "There were several strong missionary families in Hon-duras. I remember listening eagerly to the conversations, espe-cially among the missionary men as they discussed how the Men-nonite church might do leadership training in Central America. During one of our discussions, Amzie Yoder asked why didn't I go home and get a seminary degree." Although it was over-whelming, the suggestion meshed with Janet's growing desire to study and understand the Bible.

Far away from her home community's ongoing debate about the proper place for women, Janet decided to take the plunge. She made plans to move to the States and attend the As-sociated Mennonite Biblical Seminaries (AMBS) in Elkhart, In-diana. "Amzie was from the Elkhart area, and he helped me work through the application process. I recognize that I owe a lot to his encouragement." Back home in Lancaster, though, Janet's road to change met a sharp detour.

Although she was accepted at AMBS for the Spring 1978 term, she also got an invitation to return to Lancaster Mennonite High School as director of housing. "I had a decision to make. I really wanted to stay close to my family and learn to know my nieces and nephews." The signs that appeared so clear in Honduras were lost in low clouds of personal introspection as Janet asked herself, "As a woman, can or should I be doing this? I was pretty terrified about being from conservative Lancaster and going to what I then thought was liberal Elkhart." The seminary dream was not forgotten, but it took a two-year hiatus.

During those years in Lancaster County, Janet came face-to-face with her own culture's expectations of women. As an LMHS faculty member, she was caught in the maelstrom of change that finally reached the campus between 1978 and 1980. As the school's conservative founders gave way to a new generation of leaders, many students complained vehemently about the remaining vestiges of proper Mennonite actions and clothing. In particular, the head covering for women became a volatile point of concern. Young women poured out of the classrooms at 3:10 p.m. each day, removing the small round veilings from their heads as they filed into waiting school buses. Several women wrote letters of protest to the board of trustees, asking them to relax the rule.

Finally, one student simply refused to comply, coming to school without a covering. Under pressure, the trustees revised their rule. By the spring of 1980, only twenty-two percent of the women at LMS wore the long-treasured head veiling.[7]

"This strict interpretation of the whole headship idea that men were over women; that we needed to have our hair long and keep it covered as an honor to the angels or to men," says Janet. "I never was quite clear how that worked. Those verses from Paul in I Corinthians are difficult. For me they kept bringing up questions about whether I as a woman could legitimately go to seminary. But I really wanted to go, and I was being encouraged. So I left the confusion at LMHS behind, moved to Indiana, and started classes at AMBS."

The low-lying clouds cleared from Janet's horizon. She discovered kindred spirits in the women and men at the seminary. "I was sure I couldn't handle the theological vocabulary and concepts. I was certain I would feel like a fish out of water. I remember I completely lost my appetite the first weeks and had to force myself to eat. But I soon found great friends, people who are still close to me. The professors were wonderful, human, very stimulating people. I loved studying and didn't want to leave after one year as I had planned."

Around this time, Eastern Board approached Janet about returning to Honduras. The mission board would pay her second year of seminary if she then went back to Honduras under their auspices. In seminary it became obvious to Janet that she wanted to work in leadership training. She did an internship as a student pastor at St. John's United Church of Christ in Elkhart, occasionally preaching Sunday morning sermons.

By March 1983, Janet was on her way back to La Ceiba with an assignment from Eastern Board to work in leadership training and theological education.[8] The irony of a community with no credentialed women leaders sending one of its women to train Latin American pastors and lay people in church leadership cannot be taken lightly. This sharp distinction between practice and theory was bound to come up sooner or later for both the Bishop Board and Eastern Board.

Meanwhile, distance from the concerns and questions about Lancaster Mennonite women in leadership revived Janet's soul and spirit. Her periodic reports from La Ceiba displayed a high degree of personal happiness and professional satisfaction. She was obviously doing what she loved.

In 1987 Janet was invited to become director of the Bible Institute at La Ceiba. When that transition happened, the Eastern Board's Norman Shenk asked the Bishop Board for permission to license or ordain Janet. "I informed the bishops of her new title and told them that if we were sending a man to do leadership training in Honduras, we would ordain him," says Norman. "Janet was trained in our seminary, I told them, and she should be ordained."[9]

As was expected, the request attracted the board's attention. Their November 19, 1987, minutes convey a striking ambiguity in the face of this difficult inquiry. "A question was raised whether Janet Breneman should be credentialed in view of her assignment by Eastern Board as an instructor in leadership training in Honduras. There was much discussion to clarify the need and understand the circumstances of the assignment."

Some bishops voiced discomfort at the thought of ordaining a woman, while others argued that Janet had given her life to church work and deserved some recognition for her commitment. In the end, the board reminded itself that they could not ordain her. But in a truly amazing set of circumstances, they agreed to prepare a special letter of credentialing. Action II of the November 19 minutes directed the secretary "to ask representatives of the Conference Officers, the Mission Board, the fraternal representative, and Janet's conference district to develop a certificate or letter to provide a credential for Janet Breneman for her assignment in Honduras."[10]

Although she was not licensed or ordained through the normal Lancaster Conference channels, Janet Breneman received a certificate of ministry signed by the moderator of the Lancaster Conference Bishop Board in 1987. "After that, I was licensed as a minister by the Honduras Mennonite Church. That license stood for the duration of my work in Honduras," she says.

From 1987 to 1991, Janet guided the La Ceiba Bible Institute as it converted back to an extension program rather than a residential one. The Honduras Mennonite Church requested that the institute's Bible curriculum become an extension program, capable of reaching many more people in the widely scattered church communities. "We wanted to reach potential leaders in rural areas all across Honduras. I loved the work, pulling together teachers, forming groups in the different regions, and planning the courses. I've often said if I had been in my own country and doing a work I enjoyed that much, I would definitely have tried to stay with it. But it seemed like our role was to turn leadership over to the nationals as soon as possible."

As planned, Janet prepared to relinquish leadership of the Mennonite Bible Institute's extension program at La Ceiba to José Angel Ochoa. Prior to the transfer, she went through a period of intense soul-searching. What would be her next job? Had the time come to leave Central America? Had she done what she could? She had been in Honduras for most of the previous fifteen years. Perhaps it was time to go home. In a June 1989 letter to her loyal supporters at Masonville, Janet asked her family and friends to pray with her as she prepared to make a decision about whether or not she would return to Honduras after her Christmas 1989 furlough.

In what can only be described as a remarkable pattern of affirmation and direction, she received an invitation from the leaders of SEMILLA (Seminario Anabautista Latinoamericano), based in Guatemala City, to come and work for them. A unified leadership training effort of ten Central American Mennonite and Brethren in Christ national church organizations, SEMILLA envisioned and designed its seminary curriculum "conscientiously in and from a Latin American context and perspective."[11]

The tone of Janet's December 1990 letter home was considerably more focused and upbeat. "My biggest challenge and biggest joy [this past year] was working with José. I will terminate in February 1991, come home to the Lancaster area for a month, and return to work with SEMILLA beginning in April 1991."[12]

Because she transferred from a small seaside town to a tumultuous urban center, the move to Guatemala was not easy, but it brought Janet closer to two women who have become treasured friends. Janet first met Leonor Mendez, a native of Guatemala, and her husband, Mario, when they took an assignment with the Honduras Mennonite Church in the mid-1970s. When Janet moved to Guatemala's busy capital city, she reconnected to the family. "Leonor is a pastoral person and an excellent preacher. She and her family are among my dearest friends in Guatemala City. I usually spend Christmas in their home as one of the family." A visionary who has served on the Mennonite World Conference executive committee, Leonor Mendez preached one of the main evening sermons at the 1990 World Conference in Winnipeg, Manitoba.

The move to Guatemala brought Janet closer to Linda Witmer, who was also a single Eastern Board worker from Lancaster County. In June 1991, Linda returned to San Pedro Carcha, about four hours northeast of the capital, where she worked with the K'ekchi Mennonite Church as a nurse educator and administrator. Being close to Linda mellowed many of the tough days for Janet. As they built on their longtime friendship, the two women came to share a deep spiritual bond.

Several years before, Janet and Linda had both joined a newly formed women's support group. Originally organized to bring together those committed to serving the poor, the Women's Support Circle evolved into a close-knit accountability and friendship structure. Today it provides a sense of belonging, a fountain of emotional and spiritual nurture to women who have voluntarily given their lives to serving the church often in places far removed from their families of origin and home church communities.[13] The women, all of whom are committed to mutual openness, communicate through every-other-week letters and occasional retreats. Although they live on three different continents—Africa, North America, and South America—they've managed to cement relationships in a close circle of care. In addition to the larger network, each woman has her own spiritual friend and prayer partner.

Janet and Linda are prayer partners. They meet regularly and undergird each other through times of calm and storm. As intimate friends, they depend on reciprocal honesty and respect, opening windows to each other's longings as they ponder how best to be faithful. They and the other Support Circle women write to each other and get together because they enjoy the communion, because they love the security of being accountable, and because they believe in integrating the spiritual and social sides of life.

Janet explains, "I don't like how people separate spiritual life from material life. I believe the natural and spiritual are all very much one. As a church leader, I want an integrated life and witness. The Support Circle helps hold me accountable to this desire." In the way that family members often point out both negative and positive elements of each other's lives, the women of this circle sometimes challenge each other, but they also champion each other's contributions and gifts.

Witness Linda Witmer's comments about Janet Breneman. "Janet is a role model and mentor to many Central American Mennonite women. She is constantly encouraging women to use their gifts in the church. Because she presents the questions in a nonthreatening way, Janet has helped transform many Latin American Mennonite ideas about women and the church. She encouraged the administration and staff at SEMILLA to be more inclusive in their language. I know SEMILLA is different in relation to women because Janet works there."[14]

As director of SEMILLA's Basic Education Department, Janet travels throughout Latin America, editing, preparing, and putting into place educational materials for congregations and Bible institutes. As Linda reminds her, she also preaches and teaches in churches throughout the region. "Janet is an excellent Bible teacher. She makes the Scriptures come alive. She is very creative."[15]

Janet's recent editorial ventures include a thirteen-session women's study guide written by six writers, most of whom are Guatemalan, titled *Los Problemas Económicos Nos Agobian* ("The Economic Problems Are Wearing Us Out"). Another project is a massive Latin American Anabaptist Bible curriculum for children. "We are in the process of training and working with writers as they produce material. The finished product will be a church-based, nine-year curriculum in three cycles," explains Janet. "We want it to be free of frills, easy to use, and simple. We also want it to be Bible-based and Anabaptist in its focus. There is such a great need for this. Currently, our Latin American Mennonite churches use translated material written in North America. Much of it is not Anabaptist. We need our own curriculum."

Janet Breneman's projects and visions have brought dignity and hope to women and men in many of the communities of this sometimes troubled region of the world. She shares her modest Guatemala City apartment with a cat named Terremoto, moving around the city with relative comfort and ease. "Yes, it's a city that has more than its share of violence. But I don't live in a state of fear. Many cities, even in North America, deal with outbreaks of violence."

Thanks perhaps to her parents and their sense of connection and roots, Janet also returns to Masonville whenever she has a furlough. Through the years, she's given many talks and sermons to the people of this western Lancaster County congregation that nurtured her so well.

Sylvia Shirk Charles

14

Blessed by the Church

Sylvia Shirk Charles
Goshen, Indiana

IT WAS SUMMER 1954. Sylvia Shirk was three. Her parents, Frank and Erica Hege Shirk, packed up three young daughters, Louise, Sylvia, and Hilda, boarded the USS United States, and sailed from New York bound for a tiny Alsatian Mennonite community in the far northeast corner of France. They were going home. Home to the Hege family, whose magnificent farmhouse had been bombed twice during World War II. Home to Schafbusch where Erica was born and raised, where she met and married a young Lancaster County man who had come to nearby Wissembourg as a Mennonite Central Committee volunteer.[1] Home to introduce Erica's parents to their grandchildren.

The Shirk family stayed in the Alsace four months, helping the Heges move from makeshift postwar quarters to their house, which had taken nine years to rebuild. Erica's voice registers hope and memory. "I thought it was so nice that I could be there to help move into the new place. The girls had a good time with their grandparents and other relatives. I remember being surprised at how quickly Sylvia spoke Alsatian. She learned enough that first time when she was three to pick the language up quickly on our next trip in 1961."[2]

Whether it was speaking both Alsatian and English, identifying with Lancaster Mennonite and French Mennonite grandparents, or learning from cross-cultural parents, Sylvia's early years were filled with the richness that comes from recognizing goodness inherent in different ways. "The way I felt about national identity and war was certainly affected by my mother's experience," says Sylvia. "Knowing I had family and friends, people we cared about, who lived in another country made it hard for me to feel America was the best place to live."

Sylvia says that her mother's experiences relativized her own feelings about the United States. She recalls one time, while playing with an elementary school friend, that the little girl said, "Let's play like the Germans are coming. We have to take cover because they're going to bomb."

"I looked at her and said, 'The Germans!? It was the *Americans* who bombed my grandparents' farm,'" says Sylvia. "We were probably in fourth grade. I remember thinking if there was another war, I couldn't take sides the way my friend did. And that was interesting because this friend's father had been in England as a military person. Like my father, he married a woman from another country. So we had the common experience of being raised by mothers with strange accents. The difference was my friend's father had been involved in war and mine in making peace. That was how I saw it."[3]

How Sylvia saw the world was always colored by the diverse experiences, but similar views, of her Mennonite parents. In one way, her childhood and youth were very insular. "We had our Mennonite summer camp, bought groceries from a Mennonite, shopped at Harry Good's store. Our car was insured by a Mennonite insurance company, bought from a Mennonite Chevy dealer, and sold later to a Mennonite used car dealer."[4] This immersion in Lancaster Mennonite society posed both questions and answers for Sylvia Shirk.

When she was seven, her father was chosen by lot and ordained to the pastoral ministry. The ordination, held on New

Year's Eve Day in 1958 at the nearby New Holland meeting-house, made an impression on young Sylvia. "It was solemn and awesome—and kind of exciting for me because afterwards our family was just showered with attention. People brought us stuff. They paid attention to us children in positive ways, especially at the beginning."

The Shirk family's New Holland-area neighbors were following a custom familiar to many tightly knit Mennonite communities. Because their new pastor would not receive a regular paycheck for his church work, the people of the congregation reached out with other kinds of support. The women's sewing circle made quilts for Sylvia and her sisters. One farmer gave the Shirk family all the eggs and milk they needed for many years. A local businessman regularly filled the gas tank of Frank's car. In return, Frank and Erica often went far beyond the second mile to meet the growing community's spiritual needs. This kind of mutual generosity helped Sylvia feel good about the somewhat provincial, and even isolated, Mennonite world she called home.

In other ways, her opportunities were wide. Frank and Erica decided to send their children to public schools. They were not wealthy. So they saved what might have gone toward private school tuition and gave each of their nine children a special seventeenth birthday gift: a whole summer with the Hege relatives in the Alsace. Louise was first to go in 1967. Sylvia's turn came between her junior and senior year of high school, the summer of 1968. It was a chance to learn about another way to be faithful, to view the world from a European perspective, and to observe a different set of Mennonite cultural practices.

Back home at Conestoga Valley High School, Sylvia cultivated lots of friends from outside the Mennonite circle. She sang alto in the school chorus and played cello in the orchestra. She wore her hair up with a round netted covering, making her the drama teacher's obvious choice to portray an Amish girl in *Satin and Strudel*, the 1969 senior class play. "In the play, I had to let my hair down and kiss one of the most popular guys in my senior class," recalls Sylvia. "Something about that experience both fulfilled my teenage fantasies as a conservative Mennonite girl and prefigured my later departure from the more legalistic aspects of the community where I grew up. The play was, I think, symbolic of my own life."

Sylvia's high school and young adult years were happy years. They were also years filled with questions as she began to work through the complexities of balancing her narrow Mennonite experience with a much broader awareness of God's grace and mercy. "I remember coming back from my summer in the Alsace and thinking this teaching about the women's prayer veiling doesn't add up. There's no way I'm willing to say that my grandmother's faith is not real or that she is not a totally sincere Christian just because she doesn't dress a certain way or wear a covering." Sylvia became more and more certain that faithfulness was not necessarily defined by wearing a covering or by squelching her keenly felt leadership gifts.

In a fascinating twist, she learned that the French relatives she considered progressive could also be conservative. "In some ways, the Mennonites in France resemble the Mennonites in Lancaster Conference. Actually, they match quite well theologically. There are no ordained women in the French Mennonite Conference [in the spring of 1998]. Every time I go, I raise the question, 'Where are you on this?' My relatives acknowledge the French Mennonites aren't moving very fast toward having women pastors even though there are many women lay leaders, including my mother's sister, Louise Nussbaumer."

As early as age twelve, Sylvia began to use her own leadership skills at New Holland Mennonite Church. "I asked the Sunday school superintendent if there was anything I could do, and they found a job for me." The superintendent invited Sylvia to coordinate the children's story time. In the years that followed, she taught children's classes, helped guide youth activities, and agreed to several terms with a committee that planned Sunday evening worship. "I think that's when I observed that until you got to be an adult, there was equal opportunity in that church for boys and girls to be leaders."

Although her mentors and parents supported her gifts, the suggestion of future leadership in the church never came up. "I remember overhearing a conversation between a woman from our church and my parents. She said her daughter had asked whether women could be ministers in the church." Everybody chuckled in an "of course not" kind of way, Sylvia relates. "I sort of thought the same. I had never heard of that either. In fact, I think I was in college before I ever laid eyes on a woman minister."

The woman minister who caught Sylvia's eyes stood in the pulpit of a small-town Protestant church in Steinseltz, France. Sylvia had gone back to the Alsace through the Brethren Colleges Abroad program, enrolling at the University of Strasbourg for a year and commuting the short distance to stay with her grandparents, aunts, and uncles on most holidays and weekends. Watching this pastor conduct the Christmas Eve service seemed to Sylvia as right as it seemed strange. Although the occasion etched itself in her memory—much like the earlier image of the little girl who asked whether women could be ministers—Sylvia Shirk was carefree and young. She was not ready to seriously entertain the notion that she might one day be a church leader herself.

Instead, she returned to Goshen College to finish a degree in social work. After graduation, she started dating Robert Charles. "We had been friends, but the relationship developed while he was managing a coffee house in Elkhart. I had a job as a caseworker with the Elkhart County Welfare Department, and I liked to stop by the coffee shop."

On September 20, 1975, Sylvia and Robert were married at the Sermon on the Mount Chapel in Elkhart, Indiana. She transferred her membership from New Holland to East Goshen Mennonite Church, Robert's home congregation. As surely as her mother had left the Alsace, Sylvia Shirk Charles had left New Holland and the Lancaster Mennonite community.

"I hope I've clearly said how grateful I am to the Lancaster Conference for my grounding in spiritual nurture," Sylvia is careful to clarify. "I think of it as having been a nurturing place to grow up. The disappointment I've felt comes from not having women's leadership gifts embraced."

It was a disappointment Sylvia noted but never permitted to consume or limit her own dreams. She and Robert spent the first year of their marriage in the Alsace, where he studied at the University of Strasbourg and Sylvia volunteered in a children's home operated by the French Mennonites. Three summers after their wedding, they were back in northern Indiana when Sylvia gave birth to their first child on July 14, 1978.

The Sunday of Laura's birth, Sylvia's parents, Frank and Erica, slowly made room for two new realities. On the day they became grandparents for the first time, Frank was also ordained bishop to serve the Groffdale District. Erica shakes her head and explains the unusual coming together of life events. "That was such a busy week. We had the ordination. And it was at the time of the Mennonite World Conference in Wichita, so we had so many European visitors. Then I took the train to Goshen to help Sylvia with Laura, our first grandchild."

Settled and steadier days soon returned. After her mother went back home, Sylvia returned to her job as resident hall director at Goshen College. "I could do much of the work at home so Laura could be with me. Robert and I have been fortunate to have jobs that adapted fairly easily to our children and their needs. Both of us have always worked outside the home." Dan was born three days before Christmas 1980, and Sophie two days before Robert and Sylvia's seventh wedding anniversary in September 1982.

By the time of Dan's birth, the Shirk Charles family had relocated to Brussels, Belgium, to fill a general missionary assignment with Mennonite Board of Missions (MBM). The light that would change how Sylvia Shirk Charles thought about her church leadership gifts was on the horizon. At first no more than a dim ray, it was absorbed by other responsibilities, in spite of invitations like the one from her colleague, Wilda Otto. "The Christian Women of Belgium are holding a World Day of Prayer service this Thursday," Wilda asked. "Would you like to go?"[5]

Dan was only four months old, Laura was a busy two-year-old, and Sylvia had more than enough to do. Furthermore, she wasn't quite thirty, and a World Day of Prayer service seemed like an activity for old folks—an annual Christian observance which, in her memory, had usually been planned by Mennonite women's sewing circles. It was not something a budding feminist of the Baby Boom generation would be interested in. She passed on the invitation, but the light continued to rise, slowly re-coloring her experience.

When Sylvia and Robert agreed to go to Brussels, they understood that their job description included building connections to the earlier work of Mennonites in Belgium. In addition, they and their colleagues founded the Brussels Mennonite Center complete with a well-stocked children's peace library and programs to promote peace education for adults. Both Sylvia and Robert worked nearly full-time for the church. They traded child-care responsibilities, moving in tandem to do their MBM-related work while providing security for their growing family.

Given their allegiance to mutuality, Sylvia and Robert reacted with immediate concern when they learned that the deeply traditional men on the Belgian Mennonite Council preferred not to have women attend their meetings. "We had come from North America with a mandate to collaborate with the Mennonite Council. I did not expect them to object to meeting with me," recalls Sylvia. "But Belgium proved to be no different from the Mennonite church in which I had grown up. It too drew lines—to exclude women from decision making."[6] Sylvia began to ask whether Christian feminism existed in Brussels and was directed once again to the Christian Women of Belgium.

To her pleasant surprise, these women were committed to ecumenical cooperation among Catholics and Protestants, providing a space outside male-dominated structures for women leaders to grow. Sylvia embraced their cause and accepted leadership roles in the organization. Because she had taken seminary courses through the years, the group asked her to preach at the 1987 centennial celebration of World Day of Prayer. Many leaders from the various Belgian church hierarchies gathered at Saint Michael's Cathedral where they heard a small-town Lancaster County Mennonite woman address the crowd. "Since then, I have completed seminary and am employed in pastoral work," Sylvia wrote recently. "Whenever sermon delivery makes me nervous, I need only recall that day in the crowded cathedral to regain confidence."[7]

An inner desire to be a church leader had by this time moved to the conscious part of Sylvia's mind and soul. "Very gradually I had started thinking, 'Yeah, I'd like to be a pastor someday.' In Brussels I began saying it aloud."

In 1988 Sylvia and Robert begam a two-year study leave in the U.S. They moved to Somerville, Massachusetts, and Robert pursued a graduate degree in international relations at the Fletcher School of Law and Diplomacy, Tufts University. Sylvia took a full-time position at a social service agency. When asked, she also agreed to volunteer her services as pastor of the Mennonite Congregation of Boston. "That was a very positive experience for me."

During their first year in Somerville, Sylvia and Robert learned that they would not return to an assignment in Belgium. "We had to re-orient ourselves to staying in the U.S. That's when I said, 'Ah, now the time is right. Go to seminary. Finish that degree as fast as possible.'" Sylvia enrolled at the Episcopal Divinity School (EDS), a school with links to a consortium of seminaries in the Boston area. She took a class at Harvard, graduating from EDS in 1990 with an M.A. in theology.

As a member of the 1990s Mennonite Church, Sylvia Shirk Charles held impressive credentials in a denomination that was rapidly mainstreaming itself. Many opinion makers in the community were urgently trying to shed the larger society's stereotype that they were plain folks who drove horses and buggies. Mennonite Media Ministries even placed a series of 1992 advertisements in magazines such as *Newsweek* and *Time* addressing specific "Mennonite myths." One ad proclaimed, "Ask some Mennonites to hitch up a horse and buggy, and you'll either have a confused horse, or a very strange ride." A large photograph of a horse hitched backwards to a buggy dominated a smaller image of a cluster of people from various ethnic groups, none of whom were archetypal plain folks. The ad's message continued, "To be a Mennonite you just have to be committed to Jesus Christ and His people. It's as simple, as hard, and as complicated as that."[8] Like the Old World Mennonites of France, many Mennonites in the New World wished to blend more easily into local culture.

"By the time I was finished with my year at EDS, I had no doubt in my mind that I wanted to be a minister," says Sylvia. "I was a minister, and I was ready to look for full-time work in that area." In October 1992, Sylvia began a pastorate at Waterford, a Goshen-area congregation of over three hundred members in the Indiana-Michigan Conference. With Robert and the children, she headed cross-country from the Boston area to Waterford, where she was licensed as a pastor and joined a team of three ministers.

Indiana-Michigan Conference's policies provided for new pastors to be licensed for two-year terms. If all was well, a review process would lead to ordination at the end of the first term. Traditionally, this conference and several others in the Midwest have been considered more open-minded and progressive, especially when cast against the doctrine and theology of the Lancaster Mennonite Conference. Knowing that women had already been ordained in Indiana-Michigan, Sylvia expected a relatively smooth transition.

Meanwhile, back in Lancaster, Frank and Erica were observing their daughter from afar and marveling at the direction and tenacity of her vision. In the late 1980s Frank, with two other Lancaster-area bishops, researched and wrote a careful analysis of the ministry of women, leading to the licensing of the conference's first deaconess in January 1987.

Erica also began to adjust her sights. Just as it had been hard for her to accept the 1948 Lancaster Conference's unbending request that she wear a covering, it was now difficult to watch this same community accept doctrines and theology that some members of her Alsatian family even considered too liberal. "But as we watched Sylvia leading in Boston and Brussels, as we saw her gifts evolve, we became ready for ordination. I also got much encouragement from my sister Louise. She helped me think about what it might be like to see Sylvia being ordained. Hearing from both Louise and Sylvia about their work and watching them in action helped us evaluate the question of women being ordained. We became ready."

Grateful to be working in a stable environment, Sylvia settled into a routine. At the end of the required two years, a process leading toward ordination began. But all was not well. Her country church south of Goshen had its own deeply held traditions, its own legitimate questions about ordination and the meanings this ordinance might have for women and men in Christian ministry. Some folks at Waterford opposed the concept of ordination, considering it an outmoded practice. The somewhat youthful congregation had never hosted an ordination, relying on commissioned or licensed leaders and pastors who were ordained before joining the Waterford team.

Others in the congregation objected to women in church leadership and welcomed the opportunity to restate their positions more clearly. To give everyone more time, the conference minister decided Sylvia should be re-licensed, rather than ordained, for another two years. "We hurt with her," is how Erica Shirk describes this stage of her daughter's journey.

Sylvia admitted her disappointment but returned to the tasks of leading. "The congregation took some time to look at what ordination meant. I wouldn't say we reached unanimity, but I believe people began to understand why it was important to me," she says. "As a pastoral team, we also decided to study all the articles of the newly released 1995 Mennonite Confession of Faith, including the one about women in leadership. There was movement. Certain people started saying, 'We don't want a team without a woman. Having a woman pastor is very important to us.'"

In December 1995, Sylvia responded to an inquiry from Goshen College. She interviewed for the campus minister position and got the job. In the spring of 1996, she gave notice of her intentions to leave the Waterford pastorate. "When the congregation heard this, there was a burst of energy. I think they realized if they didn't act, I would leave and still not be ordained.

Some people at Waterford would have had regrets about that. As it turned out, I had my ordination June 29 and my farewell June 30."

June 29, 1996: in an uncommon gathering at an uncommon country church, people came together to witness an event that most pastors, no matter their denomination or gender, describe with awe-filled voices and a hushed sense of treading on holy ground. "Two people spoke at my ordination—my dad and a woman who had been my mentor, Martha Smith Good. The charge was given by Charlotte Holsopple Glick, a former pastor at Waterford, and Rachel Fisher, a retired minister and our overseer. To have these people, who had been supportive of me in such different ways, together in one place was very exciting. There was something very empowering about having a public ordination. I felt blessed by the church."

Blessed by the church. That longing—planted in the heart of a twelve-year-old girl during Sunday school story time—was finally satisfied. Sylvia Shirk Charles was forty-five years old with an invigorating new job. The future, with its reservoir of freedom and opportunity, lay ahead.

"Some people wonder how a Lancaster Conference bishop accepted the ordination of his daughter," says her father, Frank. "When I look at Sylvia, I know she is gifted. I'm pleased that Indiana-Michigan has recognized her gifts. It has also been good to hear her preach in New Holland, her home congregation."[9]

Notes

Chapter 1, Pages 19-36

1. Gleaned from a collection of letters Amanda Musselman wrote to her family throughout her years as a mission worker in Philadelphia. The letters were saved by her sister, Katie Musselman Myers, and deposited in the Lancaster Mennonite Historical Society Archives (LMHS) as the Amanda Musselman Collection (hereinafter called AMC).

2. Interview between the author and Ruth Myers Wyble, daughter of Amanda's sister Katie, January 15, 1998. Ruth was born in 1911 and remembers Amanda very clearly. "The reason I know she had red hair was because her brother (my uncle Eli) used to tease her about being a redhead. He ended up having four children with bright red hair. My mother always had a good laugh over that."

Also an interview between A. Grace Wenger and Ruth Myers Wyble, August 1980. Cited in A. Grace Wenger, "Amanda Musselman, 1869-1940," *Pennsylvania Mennonite Heritage* (October 1982): 2. At this time Groffdale only had services twice a month rather than every Sunday. Amanda may have attended other nearby congregations on the off Sundays.

3. Ruth Myers Wyble places Amanda at the party in her August 1980 interview with A. Grace Wenger.

4. Wyble interview, January 15, 1998. "Aunt Amanda loved beautiful clothing. My mother always said she knew how to dress. Even after I knew her when she was plain, she was so neat, such a perfectionist about her clothing." Extant photograph of Amanda Musselman, AMC, Archives of LMHS.

5. Mark R. Wenger, "Ripe Harvest: A. D. Wenger and the Birth of the Revival Movement in Lancaster Conference," *Pennsylvania Mennonite Heritage* (April 1981): 12; Joseph C. Shenk, *Silver Thread: The Ups and Downs of a Mennonite Family in Mission* (Intercourse, Pa.: Good Books, 1996), 14.

6. A. Grace Wenger, "Amanda Musselman, 1869-1940," 4.

7. Ira D. Landis, *The Missionary Movement among Lancaster Conference Mennonites* (Scottdale, Pa.: Mennonite Publishing House, 1937), 43.

8. John H. Mellinger, "The Philadelphia Mission," *Herald of Truth* (August 15, 1899), 247.

9. Mary Denlinger, "Taking a Backward Look," *Missionary Messenger* (December 1949), 4.

10. Wyble interview, January 15, 1998; Wenger, "Amanda Musselman, 1869-1940," 5.

11. Letter to Katie Myers, June 13-14, 1899, AMC, Archives of LMHS.

12. One such letter is an August 19, 1904, letter to Jacob and Mary Musselman, AMC, Archives of LMHS. This is written in epistle style with lots of quotations directly from Scripture.

13. Letter to Jacob and Mary Musselman, July 21, 1905, AMC, Archives of LMHS.

14. Letter to Mary Musselman, August 9, 1916, AMC, Archives of LMHS.

15. Letter to Katie Myers, February 13, 1902, envelope dated 1903, AMC, Archives of LMHS.

16. Wyble interview, January 15, 1998.

17. Wenger, "Amanda Musselman, 1869-1940," 7.

18. J. D. Mininger, "Mennonite Home Mission," *Herald of Truth* (November 1, 1902).

19. Interview between the author and A. Grace Wenger, January 8, 1998. Grace and her sister, Edna K. Wenger, have done extensive research on Lancaster Conference Mennonites. Grace graciously agreed to answer many different questions about Lancaster Mennonite women. Edna was in failing health but sat nearby during the interview. This interview will be cited throughout the manuscript.

20. Mellinger, 247.

21. Several of Amanda's letters home refer to visits she and Mary made to both Lancaster and Franconia congregations, AMC, Archives of LMHS.

22. "Sunday School Items: Weaverland, Pa.," *Herald of Truth* (July 15, 1899), 217.

23. Various letters offer thanks for gifts, AMC, Archives of LMHS. The sister workers also wrote regular reports for *Herald of Truth* from 1899 to 1924. In their reports, they frequently acknowledged both general and specific gifts.

24. A. Grace Wenger interview, January 8, 1998.

25. Letters to Katie Myers, March 2, 1900, and March 19, 1900, AMC, Archives of LMHS.

26. Lina Z. Ressler, "Amanda Musselman: An Appreciation," *Gospel Herald* (May 1, 1941), 120.

27. Landis, 43-44. The sixtieth-anniversary bulletin for Norris

Square Mennonite Church, June 14, 1959, lists the dates and addresses of the three different buildings used by the Philadelphia Home Mission. A copy of this bulletin found in one of the boxes labeled "Emma Rudy," Diamond Street Mennonite Church collection, Archives of LMHS.

28. Letter to Jacob and Mary Musselman, June 17, 1910, AMC, Archives of LMHS.

29. Wyble interview, January 15, 1998.

30. A. M. Eash, "A Farewell Message," *Gospel Herald* (July 10, 1919), 269.

31. The minutes and related notes of both the Lancaster Mennonite Sunday School Mission (Sunday School Mission) and the Eastern Mennonite Board of Missions and Charities (Eastern Board) are housed in the Archives of LMHS. These records are kept in boxes labeled "Eastern Board Beginnings, Record Books and Minutes" (hereinafter called Eastern Board Beginnings). Most historians consider the Lancaster Sunday School Mission the forebear of the Eastern Board. This is true on one level. On another level, it is quite clear that these two organizations had differences in focus. The 1896 Lancaster Sunday School Mission was a lay movement, supported by lay leadership. The 1914 Eastern Board was founded by the Bishop Board, supported by the ordained leadership, and open to the counsel of lay leaders such as John H. Mellinger.

32. The Lancaster Conference Bishop Board began keeping a minute record of its meetings on October 3-4, 1912. Nine bishops attended this biannual meeting. For many years, the bishops met each spring and fall. By the 1990s, the minutes indicated that thirty-five to forty bishops usually attended the regular monthly meetings. Approximately twenty-five percent of the 1990s bishops were retired. The minutes of the Lancaster Mennonite Conference Bishop Board are housed in the Archives of LMHS, labeled Bishop Board Minutes (hereinafter called BBM). Available to researchers only by special permission.

33. Eastern Board Beginnings, August 11, 1914, Archives of LMHS; BBM, October 2, 1913, Archives of LMHS.

34. Eastern Board Beginnings, April 8-9, 1918, for reference to John W. Weaver address; Eastern Board Beginnings, November 5, 1919, for reference to Amos Horst statement, Archives of LMHS.

35. Postcard dated March 11, 1937, from Ira L. Hershey to Ira D. Landis says, "I have no acct. of S.S. Mission Funds after 1906 other than for the Phila. Mission Prop. which was kept separate." Eastern Board Beginnings, Archives of LMHS.

36. Letter to Katie Myers, February 28, 1910, AMC, Archives of LMHS.

37. Mary S. Denlinger, "From Our Mission Stations, Philadelphia, Pa.," *Gospel Herald*, (March 3, 1921), 979; Mary S. Denlinger, "New

Notes from Several Stations: Philadelphia, Pa." *Gospel Herald,* (May 29, 1924), 178.

38. Wenger, "Amanda Musselman, 1869-1940," 12; A. Grace Wenger interview, January 8, 1998.

39. Minutes of the eighty-seventh quarterly meeting of the Lancaster Mennonite Sunday School Mission, July 25, 1917, held at Paradise meetinghouse. Eastern Board Beginnings, Archives of LMHS.

40. The boxes labeled "Eastern Board Beginnings Records" (Archives of LMHS) have three notebooks. One holds minutes of eighty-seven quarterly meetings of Lancaster County Mennonite Sunday School Missions. One holds minutes of Eastern Mennonite Board of Missions and Charities (Eastern Board), beginning August 11, 1914. One holds Eastern Board executive committee minutes as of the first meeting January 30, 1915.

41. Mary S. Denlinger, "From Our Mission Stations, Philadelphia, Pa.," *Gospel Herald* (October 5, 1922), 541; Landis, 44.

42. Wyble interview, January 15, 1998.

43. BBM, April 10, 1924, Archives of LMHS.

44. BBM, June 20, 1924, Archives of LMHS.

45. Letter from C. M. Brackbill to Benjamin Weaver, June 27, 1924, Benjamin W. Weaver Collection, Archives of LMHS.

46. Letter from Violet Henke, et al., to Benjamin Weaver, September 23, 1924, and letter from Mrs. M. A. MacIlree to Benjamin Weaver, September 23, 1924, Benjamin W. Weaver Collection, Archives of LMHS.

47. Norris Square Mennonite Church papers, J. Paul Graybill additions, Archives of LMHS.

48. Letter to Jacob and Mary Musselman, January 28, 1910, AMC, Archives of LMHS; Mary S. Denlinger, "Strange Days at the Philadelphia Mission," *Gospel Herald* (October 31, 1918), 527. In this report, Mary mentions that a member of the mission, Emma Wieland, had contracted the flu and been cared for at Fannie Flory's home in Mummasburg, Pa.

49. Wenger, "Amanda Musselman, 1869-1940," 18.

50. Entries in Katie Myers's diary, dated June 7-17, 1940, AMC, Archives of LMHS.

51. Amanda Musselman obituary, *Gospel Herald* (July 25, 1940), 383.

Chapter 2, Pages 39-55

1. Charlotte Stauffer Shimp, *The Preacher John Stauffer Family History* (self-published, 1930), 16.

2. Joanne Hess Siegrist, *Mennonite Women of Lancaster County* (Intercourse, Pa.: Good Books, 1996), 33-34. This photo collection includes many images of nineteenth-century Mennonites. Throughout the collec-

tion, Joanne points out that one can tell whether or not the people were church members by the style of their dress. It is fascinating to note that as recently as the 1920s, many adult Mennonites, regardless of their marital status, wore fashionable clothing. But they always changed to plain clothing as soon as they became church members, sometimes just before their weddings and sometimes many years later. Evangelism of children and young people, beginning with the 1890s revival preachers, made the key difference in dress styles of Lancaster Mennonites. Once it became commonplace for young children to join church and wear plain clothing, very few Lancaster Mennonites stayed abreast of current fashions.

3. Maria Stauffer obituary, *Herald of Truth* (October 1, 1892), 303.

4. Ibid.

5. Shimp, 16.

6. Lydia S. Sauder Mellinger, "A Glimpse from the Past," *Missionary Messenger* (September 1947), 2-3.

7. Ibid.

8. "Welsh Mountain Mission," *Herald of Truth* (July 15, 1901), 218. This is a reprint of an unidentified article in the daily *Reading Eagle*.

9. Leroy Bechler, *The Black Mennonite Church in North America 1886-1986* (Scottdale, Pa.: Herald Press, 1986), 55.

10. Eastern Board Beginnings, January 12, 1895, Archives of LMHS.

11. Eastern Board Beginnings, undated minutes, appearing between October 28, 1897, and October 27, 1898, Archives of LMHS; Noah H. Mack, "Welsh Mountain Industrial Mission," (unpublished manuscript, Bishop Noah H. Mack papers, Archives of LMHS). There are many published records of the Welsh Mountain story, most of which are distinguished by the inconsistent record of Melford H. Hagler's name (he is referred to as Milton and Milford). M. H. Noah Mack knew this Presbyterian preacher well; Mack's writings call him Melford H. Hagler.

12. Martin G. Weaver, *Mennonites of Lancaster Conference* (Scottdale, Pa.: Mennonite Publishing House, 1931), 298-301; Bechler, 56.

13. Landis, 85; Weaver, 299.

14. Mack, unpublished manuscript; J. Paul Sauder, "Anecdotes (As Recalled by the Associate Editor)," *Missionary Messenger* (September 1947), 3.

15. Mellinger, 2.

16. Noah H. Mack, "Welsh Mountain Industrial Mission Notes," *Herald of Truth* (October 1, 1899), 294-295.

17. Ibid.

18. Ibid.

19. Weaver, 299.

20. Ibid., 301.

21. Mack, "Welsh Mountain Industrial Mission Notes," 294-295.

22. Josiah W. Leeds, "The Mennonite Industrial Mission, Welsh Mountain," *West Chester Daily News*, (September 23, 1903). Reprinted in *Herald of Truth* (October 8, 1903), 327-328.

23. The Sisters, "Welsh Mountain Mission," *Herald of Truth* (October 29, 1903), 350-351; Landis, 87.

24. Mellinger, 2.

25. The Sisters, 350-351.

26. Mack, "Welsh Mountain Industrial Mission Notes," 294-295.

27. Correction note regarding Welsh Mountain, *Herald of Truth* (November 15, 1901) states, "In a report from Welsh Mountain Mission in a recent issue the statement regarding the organization of Sunday School at the chapel should have been to the effect that Milford Hagler organized the school and Bro. Ira Hershey assisted him"; The Sisters, "Welsh Mountain Industrial Notes," 350-351.

28. A. Grace Wenger, "Women in Mission in Lancaster," *Missionary Messenger* (October 1989), 12-13; J. Paul Sauder, 3; Mellinger, 2-3; Shimp, 16.

29. Mellinger, 2.

30. Nancy J. Witmer, *Caring as Our Calling: The Mennonite Children's Home* (unpublished manuscript, bound and catalogued in the LMHS library), 4.

31. Unidentified newspaper clipping, Millersville Mennonite Children's Home box (hereinafter called Children's Home records), Archives of LMHS.

32. John E. Sauder, *The Millersville Mennonite Children's Home* (unpublished manuscript, Archives of LMHS), 1-2; Children's Home records, Archives of LMHS; 1913 Charter and By-laws, Mennonite Children's Home Association, Children's Home records, Archives of LMHS.

33. Interviews between Nancy J. Witmer and J. Paul Sauder, November 28, 1983, and December 12, 1983. Cited in Nancy J. Witmer, "The Mennonite Children's Home, 1909-1972," *Pennsylvania Mennonite Heritage* (October 1985): 4.

34. Photograph donated to LMHS by Bertha (Rodgers) Quigley in 1983, Children's Home records, Archives of LMHS.

35. John E. Sauder, 2; 1913 Charter and By-laws.

36. Alta Mae Erb, *Our Home Missions* (Scottdale, Pa.: Mennonite Publishing House, 1920), 149.

37. For a detailed description of the daily schedule, see John E. Sauder, 4-5; Landis, 91-95.

38. Witmer, unpublished manuscript, 8.

39. Levi Sauder, "Santa Claus," *Herald of Truth*, (December 24, 1903), 411.

40. Shimp, 16; interviews between Nancy J. Witmer and various former children, cited in Witmer, *Caring as Our Calling*, 8.

41. Ira D. Landis, "Millersville Children's Home Notes," presented at fiftieth-anniversary meeting, June 10, 1959. Cited in Witmer, "The Mennonite Children's Home, 1909-1972," 5.

42. The Workers, "Millersville, Pa. (Children's Home Letter)," *Gospel Herald* (October 17, 1918), 516.

43. Interview with H. Richard and Ruth Sauder, August 20, 1998. H. Richard is the adopted son of Levi and Lydia Sauder. His keen memory helped fill in the gaps of many parts of Lydia Sauder's life. He was born November 9, 1919, and came to the Children's Home sometime soon after that. He heard the story of the flu epidemic from his parents.

44. "15 More Local People Victims of Epidemic," *Lancaster Intelligencer Journal* (October 7, 1918), 1 and 3; "Would Bar Visits to Infected Homes," *Lancaster Intelligencer Journal* (October 7, 1918), 3.

45. Richard and Ruth Sauder interview, August 20, 1998.

46. Witmer, unpublished manuscript, 33-34.

47. Richard and Ruth Sauder interview, August 20, 1998; "Mother Gets Boys with Pistols to Kidnap Daughter," *Lancaster Intelligencer* (March 23, 1927), 1 and 4; "Release Woman on $1000 Bail in Conspiracy," *Lancaster Intelligencer* (March 24, 1927), 1 and 25.

48. "Field Notes," *Gospel Herald* (March 31, 1927), 1111; Witmer, unpublished manuscript, 6.

49. John E. Sauder, 3. John E. Sauder's words about Lydia taking charge are supported by Levi Sauder's obituary written soon after his death and published in *Gospel Herald* (December 5, 1940). The obit writer says, "During his last illness of ten weeks 'Mamma Sauder' carried on his 'desk work' and that arrangement continues for the present."

50. *Mennonite Encyclopedia*, vol. 5 (Scottdale, Pa.: Mennonite Publishing House, 1956), 553.

51. "Oreville Home Matron Dies of Heat Prostration," *Daily Intelligencer Journal* (June 28, 1952), 2.

52. Death Record Book, Papers of Jacob D. Mellinger, Archives of LMHS.

Chapter 3, Pages 57-74

1. Noah Mack papers, brown notebook/journal, Archives of LMHS.

2. The direct quotations in this chapter are taken from a tape recording of Phebe Yoder speaking to a Lancaster Mennonite School Girls' Prayer Circle, side A, and a tape recording of a more intimate conversation with several friends at Lois Keener's house, side B. Both occurred October 13, 1969. Original reel tape made and owned by Catharine Leatherman.

Cassette copy of tape donated to LMHS archives by the author. Hereinafter called Phebe Yoder tape.

3. "In Memory of Phebe Yoder," obituary written by her family September 19, 1981, and copied in funeral program. Copy of program in possession of Catharine Leatherman, March 1998, and shown to author.

4. Elaine Sommers Rich, *Mennonite Women: A Story of God's Faithfulness 1683-1983* (Scottdale, Pa.: Herald Press, 1983), 140.

5. Interview with Leah Yoder Loucks, Phebe's younger sister, March 21, 1998. This description of their farm rolled off her tongue with ease. Leah had obviously used it many times. It also made it possible for the author to find the farm, which is no longer in the Yoder family.

6. This description based on interviews with Catharine Leatherman, Grace Stauffer, Mahlon Hess, and Miriam Wenger Shenk (all conducted by the author in March 1998) and from observations of the physical features of Leah Yoder Loucks, who was described as "looking more like Phebe than any of her other siblings."

7. Interview with Miriam Wenger Shenk, March 2, 1998. Miriam and Phebe lived together in Mugango and Bukiroba, Tanzania, at different times between 1946 and 1970.

8. Phebe Yoder tape, side A.

9. Rich, 140.

10. Phebe Yoder tape, side B. Phebe recited from memory the words in Orie Miller's 1937 letter.

11. Wenger Shenk interview, March 2, 1998.

12. Grace Stauffer, "Mother to a Multitude," *Missionary Messenger* (August 1982), 3.

13. Letter from Mahlon and Mary Hess to the author, April 28, 1998.

14. Wenger Shenk interview, March 2, 1998.

15. Photo diary of Catharine Leatherman's 1988 visit to Tanzania. Shown to the author during March 5, 1998, visit.

16. Wenger Shenk interview, March 2, 1998.

17. Letter written by Phebe Yoder, December 26, 1940, for the Mary K. Zimmerman Africa mimeograph letters. This collection includes letters dated April 3, 1934-February 1952. Several complete copies are housed in boxes at the Archives of LMHS. Hereinafter called MKZ letters.

18. Wenger Shenk interview, March 2, 1998.

19. Joseph C. Shenk, *Silver Thread*, 78; Joseph C. Shenk, *Kisare: A Mennonite of Kiseru* (Salunga, Pa.: Eastern Mennonite Board of Missions and Charities, 1984), 94

20. Wenger Shenk interview, March 2, 1998; interview with Catharine Leatherman, December 19, 1997.

21. Letter from Mahlon Hess to the author, September 5, 1998.

22. Shenk, *Kisare*, 78-79; Hess letter, September 5, 1998.

23. Hess letter, September 5, 1998. Mahlon was a member of the board of directors at this time.

24. Catharine Leatherman, "Phebe—My Friend," *Missionary Messenger* (August 1982), 2.

25. MKZ letters; several letters dated November 24, 1942-July 12, 1943, refer to Phebe's Capetown furlough.

26. Wenger Shenk interview, March 2, 1998.

27. MKZ letters; various letters dated August 27, 1944-April 26, 1945, refer to the Leatherman-Yoder trek home..

28. J. Clyde Shenk, "A Woman of Prayer," *Missionary Messenger* (August 1982), 6-7; note from Catharine Leatherman to the author, September 5, 1998; MKZ letters, July 10, 1946, by Phebe Yoder.

29. Mahlon and Mary Hess letter to the author, April 28, 1998.

30. Wenger Shenk interview, March 2, 1998.

31. Hess letter, April 28, 1998.

32. Interview with Mahlon and Mary Hess, March 2, 1998.

33. Wenger Shenk interview, March 2, 1998.

34. Hess interview, March 2, 1998.

35. Phebe Yoder funeral program.

Chapter 4, Pages 77-86

1. Unless otherwise noted, all direct quotations are from an interview between the author and Minnie Eberly Holsopple Good at her home in Akron, Pennsylvania, January 22, 1998.

2. Alice W. Lapp, "Minnie Good: A Woman in Ministry," *WMSC Voice* (March 1989), 10.

3. A. Grace Wenger interview, January 8, 1998. Grace's sister, Edna K. Wenger, was in failing health. She sat and listened to our conversation but made no comments herself. Grace told this story, complete with the "gooble, gooble," to illustrate Minnie's style of speech.

4. Lapp, 10-11.

5. Interview between the author and Barbara Eberly at the home she shares with Minnie in Akron, Pennsylvania, January 22, 1998.

6. Sanford G. Shetler, *Two Centuries of Struggle and Growth, 1763-1963: A History of Allegheny Mennonite Conference* (Hollsopple, Pa.: Allegheny Mennonite Conference, 1963), 144.

7. Lapp, 11.

Chapter 5, Pages 89-99

1. The historical record indicates the *first* Bible school was held at Esther Mellinger's Hinkletown home the summer of 1934. The Hinkle-

town congregation's decision to date the plaque 1936 probably reflects the "first" summer after Esther invited her brother, Abe, and a friend, John S. Wenger, to serve as superintendents. The historical record also reflects that Esther was very much involved in planning the first Sunday morning service at Hinkletown in 1943.

2. A. Grace Wenger interview, January 8, 1998. Grace's sister, Edna K. Wenger, was Esther Mellinger's roommate at Eastern Mennonite School in 1934-35 when Esther decided to teach the children at Hinkletown. Edna and Esther remained lifelong friends, and Edna's fine 1985 history of the Hinkletown Mennonite Church is dedicated to "The memory of Esther Mellinger Bair 1909-1967 who began the first Hinkletown Summer Bible School at her home in 1934."

3. Interview with Doris Sensenig, daughter of Abe Mellinger, Esther Mellinger's brother, August 20, 1998.

4. Edna K. Wenger, *The Story of Hinkletown Mennonite Church* (Ephrata, Pa.: Hinkletown Mennonite Church, 1985), 186. A photograph on this page shows Aldus Mellinger with his oldest son, Ben, standing outside their shop with two 1914 Fords and a 1916 Reo in the background; interview with Ruth Horst Herr, January 22, 1999.

5. Edna K. Wenger, 55.

6. Ibid., 57. Esther was baptized at the end of a two-week series of meetings by evangelist I. B. Good at Ephrata Mennonite Church. During a telephone interview with Ruth Horst Herr, October 1, 1998, Ruth stated that the Mellinger family always attended Metzler Mennonite Church on Sunday mornings. "But my grandma and Aunt Esther often went to Ephrata or other local churches when there were special meetings. Esther and Abe were also involved with a young people's group at Ephrata."

7. Siegrist, 64; Edna K. Wenger, 53-55.

8. Card from Esther Mellinger to her parents, cited in Edna K. Wenger, 55.

9. Edna K. Wenger, 54.

10. Esther Mellinger as quoted in Edna K. Wenger, 53.

11. Edna K. Wenger, 53.

12. Ruth Horst Herr as quoted in Edna K. Wenger, 6.

13. Esther Mellinger's 1934 photo album, including many photos from her days at Eastern Mennonite School. Passed on to Joanne Siegrist for safekeeping. Shown to the author on August 13, 1998.

14. Edna K. Wenger, 3.

15. Edna K. Wenger, 134. A photograph on this page shows the entire Hinkletown Bible School in 1935. Every one of the sixty-two students is identified by name.

16. Clair Mellinger, as quoted in Edna K. Wenger, 6.

17. A. Grace Wenger interview, January 8, 1998. Grace overheard

Esther saying this to a friend.

18. A. Grace Wenger, *Frontiers of Faithfulness: The Story of the Groffdale Mennonite Church* (Leola, Pa.: Groffdale Mennonite Church, 1992), 150; Edna K. Wenger, 60-63.

19. Ruth Horst Herr, as quoted in Edna K. Wenger, 7.

20. Mary Good, as quoted in Edna K. Wenger, 190.

21. Esther Mellinger, "God Sometimes Shuts the Door," *Gospel Herald* (April 8, 1937), 45.

22. Ruth Horst Herr telephone interview, October 1, 1998.

23. Edna K. Wenger, 56.

24. Ibid., 8-10.

25. Ruth Horst Herr telephone interview, October 1, 1998.

26. Mary W. Wenger, *Carpenter Mennonite Church* (Talmage, Pa.: Carpenter Mennonite Church, 1979), 18.

27. Ibid.

28. Ibid., 64.

29. Edna K. Wenger, 56; Mary W. Wenger, 23.

30. Edna K. Wenger, 56.

31. Letter from Lois Mellinger Glick to Edna K. Wenger, October 11, 1984, as quoted in Edna K. Wenger, 57.

Chapter 6, Pages 101-115

1. Unless otherwise noted, all direct quotations are from interviews with Catharine Garber Leatherman, December 19, 1997, and March 5, 1998.

2. A. Grace Wenger, *A People in Mission*: 1894-1994 (Salunga, Pa.: Eastern Mennonite Missions, 1994), 54. Although Wenger does not cite a date for this interchange, it probably occurred before Elkhart transferred the Phebe Yoder tithes to Lancaster for the Eastern Board's emerging Africa work.

3. Joseph C. Shenk, *Kisare*, 66.

4. Ibid., 69.

5. MKZ letters, May 10, 1938, by Ray and Miriam Wenger.

6. Joseph C. Shenk, *Silver Thread, 108.* Photograph of the Tanganyika missionaries in 1941.

7. MKZ letters, April 26, 1945, by John Leatherman.

8. As quoted in A. Grace Wenger, *A People in Mission*, 53-54.

Chapter 7, Pages 117-126

1. As quoted in Esther Eby Glass, "Crafts Are for Personal Joy and Endless Sharing," *Christian Living* (June, 1960), 36.

2. Glass, 36.

3. Interview between the author and Melvin Lauver, November 17, 1997.

4. Melvin Lauver interview, November 17, 1997; Steven M. Nolt, "Self-Help Philosophy and Organizational Growth: The Origins and Development of SELFHELP Crafts, 1946-1970," *Pennsylvania Mennonite Heritage* (October 1991): 16.

5. Nolt, 16.

6. Ibid., 18-23.

7. A fascinating side note is that at least three women other than Mary Lauver, Olga Martens, and Edna Ruth Byler have received credit for founding SELFHELP Crafts. In 1951 an indigenous needlework project was established in Jordan. Independent from and perhaps unaware of the Puerto Rico work, MCC nurse Ruth Lederach supplied linen and thread and helped the women sell their work in Jordan. When Ruth left Jordan in 1953, management of the Jordanian project passed into the hands of Ada and Ida Stoltzfus. Edna Ruth Byler did not purchase needlework from Jordan until 1952. For more information, see Nolt, 17-23.

8. Alice Lapp, "A Ministering Spirit," *Christian Living* (April, 1990), 17-18.

9. "Minister's Wife Makes Gifts from Odds and Ends," *Intelligencer Journal* (October 30, 1958), no page numbers visible on the clipping, personal papers of Melvin Lauver (hereinafter called Lauver papers), Lititz, Pennsylvania.

10. Lapp, 18.

11. "A Dream Fulfilled—20 Years of Retreats: A Dialogue between Beulah Diffenbach and Mary Lauver," *Missionary Messenger* (May 1981), 14.

12. "Decorative Items for the Home" and "Gettysburg Sub-League Plans Program, Elections Monday" (dated May 5, 1969), two different unidentified newspaper articles, Lauver papers.

13. As quoted in Lapp, 16.

14. As quoted in Judy Shank, "Sourdough Bread Has Personality of Its Own," *Intelligencer Journal* (October 16, 1976), 11.

15. Ibid., 11.

16. Lapp, 18.

17. As quoted in Lapp, 18.

18. Lapp, 18.

Chapter 8, Pages 129-141

1. Unless otherwise noted, all direct quotations are from an interview with Jean Kraybill Shenk, November 20, 1997, or an interview with

Norman and Jean Kraybill Shenk, May 19, 1998.

2. Phil Baker-Shenk, "Norman G. and Jean K. Shenk," in *A History of the Erisman Mennonite Church*, edited by Nancy Witmer (Erisman Mennonite Church, 1991), 27-28.

3. Jean Kraybill Shenk, *The Role of Women in the Believer's Church* (unpublished manuscript, dated April 1983). Copy shown to the author September 1, 1998.

4. Letter to Noah Hershey, moderator of Lancaster Mennonite Conference, August 30, 1985. Copy of letter shown to the author September 1, 1998.

5. BBM, September 16, 1985, Archives of LMHS.

6. BBM, June 19, 1986, Archives of LMHS.

7. Letter from H. Howard Witmer, secretary of Lancaster Mennonite Conference Bishop Board, addressed "To Whom it may concern" and sent to conference congregations, December 9, 1986. Copy shown to the author on September 1, 1998.

Chapter 9, Pages 143-156

1. BBM, October 5-7, 1932, Archives of LMHS.

2. *50th Anniversary: Bowmansville Church Building, 1922-1972*, compiled by Henry W. Horning (self-published).

3. Unless otherwise noted, all direct quotations are from an interview with Lena Horning Brown, January 30, 1998, or an interview with Lena and Mike Brown, June 6, 1998.

4. Harold S. Stauffer, "Trial of Grove's Assassin," *Missionary Messenger* (January 1963), 3.

5. Letters from Harold S. Stauffer to Paul N. Kraybill, July 22, 1962, and July 25, 1962. Housed in boxes labeled African Missionary Papers, Archives of LMHS.

6. Joseph M. Hess, *Harvest on the Hill* (Camp Hill, Pa.: Slate Hill Mennonite Church, 1991), 106.

7. Connie F. Stauffer, *"I'd Do It Anyway"* (unpublished manuscript, undated, Quiet Shouts collection, Archives of LMHS), 3.

8. Ibid.

9. Minutes of the Task Force on Women in Church and Family, January 27, 1986, and March 24, 1986, currently housed at Congregational Resource Center, Lancaster Conference Offices. Eventually to be donated to Archives at LMHS. Also see BBM, February 20, 1986, Archives of LMHS.

10. Joseph M. Hess, 126.

11. BBM, February 19, 1987, Archives of LMHS.

12. Joseph M. Hess, 127.

13. Connie F. Stauffer, 5.

14. Lena and Mike Brown interview, June 6, 1998.

15. Lena Horning Brown during Sunday morning sermon at Slate Hill Mennonite Church, Camp Hill, Pennsylvania, February 8, 1998.

Chapter 10, Pages 159-169

1. Unless otherwise noted, all direct quotations are from an interview with Mattie Cooper Nikiema, Philadelphia, Pennsylvania, July 11, 1998.

2. Papers of Emma Rudy, diary entries for February 11, April 25, and April 27, 1952, Archives of LMHS. Mattie Cooper Nikiema also stated that she and her mother were received into membership sometime in 1952.

3. Robert W. Good, "Origins of the Diamond Street Mennonite Church in Philadelphia, Pennsylvania: 1942 to 1967," *Pennsylvania Mennonite Heritage* (April 1995): 24.

4. Papers of Emma Rudy, Archives of LMHS. Several photographs in this large collection show the interior of the meetinghouse from different angles.

5. Easter Jackson was excommunicated by J. Paul Graybill because of a rumor that she was having a relationship with the father of her son. In a July 1998 interview, Mattie states, "It was not true." In fact, in the 1990s Luke and Miriam Stoltzfus were led to apologize to Easter Jackson.

6. Good, 22.

7. Handwritten Record Book of Diamond Street Mennonite Church, Congregational Records of Diamond Street, Archives of LMHS. This hardbound and paginated record book has entries beginning in 1935 and ending September 9, 1968.

8. Robert W. Good, *Forty Years on Diamond Street: A Historical Research of Diamond Street Mennonite Church and Mennonite Mission to Philadelphia* (unpublished manuscript, dated February 26, 1982), 33. Bound and catalogued in the LMHS library. This manuscript has raised questions for some current and former members of Diamond Street Mennonite Church. Some of its conclusions are considered inaccurate by those who actually lived through the times when Bishop J. Paul Graybill and those who shared his views were trying to transplant plain Lancaster Mennonite culture to the heart of one of the eastern seaboard's most vibrant urban black communities.

9. Eastern Board's reply letter dated December 27, 1978, makes reference to Diamond Street's two requests in a letter written by Mattie Cooper. Diamond Street council of elders minutes dated November 19, 1978, authorize Mattie to write the letter of request. Mattie reports that she

wrote the letter at the next council meeting, dated December 14, 1978. Eastern Board's letter states, "Thanks for your letter of January 7." This appears to be a typographical error and should say, "your letter of December 7." Both Eastern Board's letter and council minutes housed in Congregational Records of Diamond Street, Archives of LMHS.

10. Good, *Forty Years*, 53. Refers to interviews with William Jackson, December 30, 1981, and Freeman Miller, December 31, 1981.

11. In a letter to Eastern Board dated July 5, 1979, Mattie writes, "We have begun discussing your suggestions in our council and have decided that with the press of other things just now we need more time to process your suggestions." She goes on to tell Eastern Board that she will be leaving on a three-year term with MCC and that future correspondence should be addressed to Freeman Miller. Congregational Records of Diamond Street, Archives of LMHS.

Chapter 11, Pages 171-184

1. Elizabeth G. Nissley, untitled autobiography, March 18, 1990, 1. From Quiet Shouts collection, Archives of LMHS.

2. Unless otherwise noted, all direct quotations are from an interview with Elizabeth Landis Nissley, October 29, 1997, or an interview with Elizabeth and Kenneth Nissley, January 21, 1998.

3. Steven M. Nolt, "Church Discipline in the Lancaster Mennonite Conference: The Printed Rules and Discipline, 1881-1968," *Pennsylvania Mennonite Heritage* (October 1992): 9-10.

4. Ibid.

5. Written copy of sermon by Libby Nissley. Shown to the author October 29, 1997.

Chapter 12, Pages 187-196

1. Unless otherwise noted, all direct quotations are from interviews with Miriam Book, October 26, 1997, and December 29, 1997.

2. Miriam Book, untitled autobiography, September 30, 1992, 1. From Quiet Shouts collection, Archives of LMHS.

3. Ibid.

Chapter 13, Pages 199-213

1. Unless otherwise noted, all direct quotations are from interviews with Janet Breneman, September 12, 1997, and September 15, 1998.

2. Mahlon M. Hess, *Gleanings from Our Past: Masonville Mennonite Church* (Washington Boro, Pa.: Masonville Mennonite Church, 1975),

8-10.

    3. Ibid., 68-69.

    4. Janet Breneman, "Letters," *Missionary Messenger* (September 1970), 19.

    5. Mahlon M. Hess, 50-56. Photographs in this 1975 book clearly show the changing dress standards at Masonville.

    6. Janet Breneman as quoted in Grace Kauffman, "A Dream Develops in Honduras," *Missionary Messenger* (April 1977), 4.

    7. Donald B. Kraybill, *Passing on the Faith: The Story of a Mennonite School* (Intercourse, Pa.: Good Books, 1991), 199-202.

    8. "To Honduras," *Missionary Messenger* (March 1983), 20. The caption under Janet's photo proclaims "leadership training/theological education."

    9. Norman and Jean Shenk interview, May 19, 1998.

    10. BBM, November 19, 1987, Archives of LMHS.

    11. Amzie Yoder, "An Emmaus Journey," *Missionary Messenger* (April 1986), 6-7.

    12. Both the June 1989 and December 1990 letters in the files of Masonville Mennonite Church, Archives of LMHS.

    13. Rose Breneman Stewart, "Supporting Each Other in Singleness, Service, and Counterculture Values," *Gospel Herald* (January 10, 1995), 6.

    14. Handwritten note from Linda Witmer to the author, September 28, 1998.

    15. Ibid.

Chapter 14, Pages 215-226

    1. Erica Hege Shirk, *One Farm, Two Wars, Three Generations* (Morgantown, Pa.: Masthof Press, 1996).

    2. Interview with Frank and Erica Shirk, June 29, 1998.

    3. Unless otherwise noted, all direct quotations are from an interview with Sylvia Shirk Charles, March 4, 1998.

    4. Sylvia Shirk Charles, "Christian Women of Belgium," in *To See Each Other's Good*, edited by Dorothy Yoder Nyce (Freeman, S.Dak.: Pine Hill Press, 1996), 53-54.

    5. As quoted by Shirk Charles in Nyce, 50.

    6. Ibid., 55.

    7. Ibid.

    8. Emerson L. Lesher, "A Campaign to End Mennonite Myths," *Festival Quarterly* (Winter 1992), 16.

    9. Frank and Erica Shirk interview, June 29, 1998.

Bibliography

Bechler, Leroy. *The Black Mennonite Church in North America 1886-1986.* Scottdale, Pa.: Herald Press, 1986.

Burkholder, Roy S. *Be Not Conformed to This World.* Morgantown, Pa.: Masthof Press, 1997.

Cummings, Mary Lou, ed. *Full Circle: Stories of Mennonite Women.* Newton, Kans.: Faith and Life Press, 1978.

Erb, Alta Mae. *Our Home Missions.* Scottdale, Pa.: Mennonite Publishing House, 1920.

Eshleman, Merle W. *Africa Answers.* Scottdale, Pa.: Mennonite Publishing House, 1951.

Fahs, Sophia Lyon. *Uganda's White Man of Work: A Story of Alexander M. Mackay.* Dayton, Ohio: Foreign Missionary Society, United Brethren in Christ, 1907.

Hess, Joseph M. *Harvest on the Hill.* Camp Hill, Pa.: Slate Hill Mennonite Church, 1991.

Hess, Mahlon M. *Gleanings from Our Past: Masonville Mennonite Church.* Washington Boro, Pa.: Masonville Mennonite Church, 1975.

Horning, Henry W, comp. *50th Anniversary: Bowmansville Church Building (1922-1972).* Bowmansville, Pa.: Bowmansville Mennonite Church, 1972.

Kraybill, Donald B. *Passing on the Faith: The Story of a Mennonite School.* Intercourse, Pa.: Good Books, 1991.

Kriss, Steve and Jewel Showalter. "A Stalwart in the Church," *Missionary Messenger* (May 1995).

Landis, Ira D. *The Missionary Movement among Lancaster Conference Mennonites.* Scottdale, Pa.: Mennonite Publishing House, 1937.

Leatherman, Catharine. *Ye Are God's Building: The Story of Twenty-Five Years in Tanganyika.* Salunga, Pa.: Eastern Mennonite Board of Missions and Charities, 1959.

Nyce, Dorothy Yoder. *To See Each Other's Good.* Freeman, S.Dak.: Pine Hill Press, 1996.

Rich, Elaine Sommers. *Mennonite Women: A Story of God's Faithfulness 1683-1983.* Scottdale, Pa.: Herald Press, 1983.

Shenk, David W. *Mennonite Safari.* Scottdale, Pa.: Herald Press, 1974.

Shenk, Joseph C. *Kisare: A Mennonite of Kiseru.* Salunga, Pa.: Eastern Mennonite Board of Missions and Charities, 1984.

———. *Silver Thread: The Ups and Downs of a Mennonite Family in Mission (1895-1995).* Intercourse, Pa.: Good Books, 1996.

Shetler, Sanford G. *Two Centuries of Struggle and Growth: 1763-1963: A History of Allegheny Mennonite Conference.* Hollsopple, Pa.: Allegheny Mennonite Conference, 1963.

Shimp, Charlotte Stauffer. *The Preacher John Stauffer Family History.* Self-published, 1930.

Shirk, Erica Hege. *One Farm, Two Wars, Three Generations.* Morgantown, Pa.: Masthof Press, 1996.

Siegrist, Joanne Hess. *Mennonite Women of Lancaster County.* Intercourse, Pa.: Good Books, 1996.

Weaver, Martin G. *Mennonites of Lancaster Conference*. Scottdale, Pa.: Mennonite Publishing House, 1931.

Wenger, A. Grace. *Frontiers of Faithfulness: The Story of the Groffdale Mennonite Church*. Leola, Pa.: Groffdale Mennonite Church, 1992.

———. *A People in Mission: 1894-1994*. Salunga, Pa.: Eastern Mennonite Missions, 1994.

Wenger, Edna K., ed. *The Story of Hinkletown Mennonite Church*. Ephrata, Pa.: Hinkletown Mennonite Church, 1985.

Wenger, Mary W. *Carpenter Mennonite Church*. Talmage, Pa.: Carpenter Mennonite Church, 1979.

Witmer, Nancy, ed. *A History of the Erisman Mennonite Church*. Mount Joy, Pa.: Erisman Mennonite Church, 1991.

Zimmerman, Ada M., and Catharine Leatherman. *Africa Calls*. Scottdale, Pa.: Mennonite Publishing House, preface dated 1936.

The Author

LOUISE STOLTZFUS LIVES IN Lancaster, Pennsylvania, where she was born ·and raised. Her family of origin was Old Order Amish, and she spends much of her professional life writing about subjects related to Amish and Mennonite life. Her most recent title is *Traces of Wisdom: Amish Women and the Pursuit of Life's Simple Pleasures* (Hyperion, 1998). She is also author of two other Amish-related books and six cookbooks, all published by Good Books 1989-1996. She is a member of Blossom Hill Mennonite Church, Lancaster.